# Scrounging the Islands with the Legendary Don the Beachcomber

# Scrounging the Islands with the Legendary Don the Beachcomber

✦

## Host to Diplomat, Beachcomber, Prince and Pirate

*Arnold Bitner*

iUniverse, Inc.

New York Lincoln Shanghai

# Scrounging the Islands with the Legendary Don the Beachcomber
## Host to Diplomat, Beachcomber, Prince and Pirate

iUniverse books may be ordered through booksellers or by contacting:

iUniverse
2021 Pine Lake Road, Suite 100
Lincoln, NE 68512
www.iuniverse.com
1-800-Authors (1-800-288-4677)

Because of the dynamic nature of the Internet, any Web addresses or links contained in this book may have changed since publication and may no longer be valid.

The views expressed in this work are solely those of the author and do not necessarily reflect the views of the publisher, and the publisher hereby disclaims any responsibility for them.

ISBN: 978-0-595-47884-2 (pbk)
ISBN: 978-0-595-60014-4 (ebk)

Printed in the United States of America

# Contents

# *Acknowledgments*

I would like to express my sincere appreciation to my wife, Phoebe Beach, who first suggested that I, instead of her, research and write the Don the Beachcomber story, and without whose editorial assistance it would have never been completed.

Also, my sincere thanks to Joseph Tirello, who from his home in the state of Tennessee, assisted in gathering and refining the information about Major Don Beach-Comber's World War II experiences in Italy, of which Joe played such an important role as Don's sidekick and interrupter.

Finally, a special thank you to Donn Beach, a.k.a. Don the Beachcomber, who found it difficult to write about himself although he was asked to do so, and tried many times. His story was so fascinating it simply sprang to life from the treasure trove of memorabilia he left behind and simply begged to be completed. I just happened to be the lucky person who was the recipient of the opportunity.

# Grandpappy and Anna Moray

It all began in 1907 on George Washington's birthday—February 22nd—in the township of Mexia, Texas. His mother named him, Ernest Raymond Beaumont Gantt.

At seven-years-old, Ernest began his wordly adventures in September of 1914 when he traveled by himself, on a bus, from Mexia to Mandeville, Louisiana to live for the first time on his grandfather's plantation near Lake Pontchartrain across from New Orleans. Later in the same month he sailed with his grandfather on his grandfather's yacht from the Port of New Orleans to Port Antonio, Jamaica in the West Indies. The exciting, exotic and romantic atmosphere of the Caribbean was to become quite familiar to the young boy, and Jamaica quickly became the scene of some of Ernest's early days of schooling. The opportunity to visit and live with family and friends in this strange, and at the time, to Ernest, far away land, added flavor and inspiration to his developing mind. It was also when he first experienced fine Jamaican Rhum.

In his own words, Don the Beachcomber describes his grandfather:

*Grandpappy often chased the young servant girls around the plantation house. I suppose he thought he was in his prime, but he was actually almost seventy. When he died, among those who knew him, none would have expected his life to have ended any other way. It's only fitting that it was a lovely belle like Anna Moray who led Grandpappy astray. The old man, that's what I often called my grandpappy, had taken an instant liking to Anna one hot afternoon while he was sipping a bottle of fine*

1

*Jamaican rhum during one of our jaunts to that lovely island. Anna was a vision if ever there was one, and I remember the day when my grand-pappy hired her away from the owner of a little Jamaican Bar. The old man had a natural twinkle in his eyes some older men seem to develop with age. It would always brighten up a women's heart and win her over. Despite Anna's obvious mixed-race beauty and winning smile, despite her perfect command of the English language, which indicated she wasn't one of her country's uneducated, and despite the fact that Anna must have had numerous suitors, both welcome and unwelcome, Anna was no different from any other woman Grandpappy took a liking to. Once he turned on the charm, Anna was his for the taking. The old man said he found it difficult to keep his hands to himself. Anna was always quick enough to tease and escape without offending, but she was more than eager to come to the United States. It was as if the two of them were brought into this world for each other. The old man's natural gift of persuasion quickly caused Anna to take him up on his offer.*

*Anna thoroughly enjoyed her first cruise through the islands of the Carribean. She had never been away from Jamaica, and she absolutely loved the view of the island as seen from out at sea. She had no idea the land in which she was born and raised looked so enchanting and invit-ing from the outside. But it wasn't only Jamaica that enthralled Anna, it was all of the islands as Grandpappy sailed his yacht from Santo Dom-ingo and San Juan to Havana and up the Florida Keys.*

*Of course, I took great pride in America, and promptly puffed up when we approached Miami. It was especially exciting this time for two reasons. Our return from previous voyages always brought us into the country through the Port of New Orleans. Not only would this be my first visit to Ponce de Leon's land of eternal life, but I had Anna standing with me at the ship's railing, listening intently, or so I thought, to my constant babble about the wonderful way of life in the deep south.*

*My grandpappy certainly was a great talker and story teller, and I suppose that's where I got my gift of gab. I marveled at his natural instinct when it came to dealing with and winning over someone, whether it be man, woman or child, whenever he came across an opportunity to make another friend. He was artistry in motion, and none of it was put on. Oh, sure, there were those times when he deliberately used his natural talent on some obnoxious human being, but only because that person had been such an ass in the first place. The old man found it much easier to win the person over to his side, and then take advantage of them, all the while making them think everything was their own idea when in actual fact it was Grandpappy all along.*

*When we reached the docks in Miami, Grandpappy gave the custom's guy a sob-story about Anna along with a C-note. Before long, the old man had purchased a new touring car and the three of us, Grandpappy, Anna and me, were bound for his plantation near Lake Pontchartrain in Cajun Country while the rest of the crew took the schooner home. It was a pleasure to watch the old man practice the art of wheeling and dealing to perfection during the winters I spent with him. It was certainly a great education in the ways of human nature.*

*Grandpappy owned an import/export business in New Orleans, but after prohibition set in he also took up rum running. Had my mother known this, I have serious doubts she would have allowed me to live with Grandpappy every winter. Grandpappy had convinced my mother that I would receive a much better education in New Orleans than in Texas. Grandpappy paid for everything I needed at school. Still, he expected just as much from me as any other member of his crew.*

*The old man knew a lot of people who thought they were his friend, but it was his drinking cronies whom he would invite out to the plantation. He played his role of a southern gentleman with charm and perfection. His thin, but muscular six foot frame, was always dressed in the whitest of white suits money could buy. His equally white plantation hat sat properly tilted on his head, his naturally white hair sticking out around the edges, his white goatee and mustache perfectly trimmed, his walking cane always at his side. Grandpappy told me his hair began to turn white when he was in his early thirties. He'd copied his style from photographs, and used it strictly for effect. His image was perfect, and it certainly matched his wonderful, even magical, personality.*

*The old man and his cronies would get together by the oyster beds along the bank of the Mississippi River. Each guest would be given waders, an apron with small pockets in the front containing fresh limes, picant sauce and an oyster knife. They would wade out into the river, reach down for the fresh oysters, haul them up, add the condiments and wash them down with Grandpappy's special recipe for mint juleps. The whiskey had been aged for almost a month in an old wooden bucket that had not been washed out since the day it was purchased. The mint, of course, was always freshly picked from the garden that morning. Along with fine Cuban cigars, the mint juleps were served by Anna and two of the other girls on large, fine silver platters.*

*Anna could easily outrun Grandpappy, but she loved to tease and playfully torment the old man. She would run just fast enough to keep my grandpappy at bay until they had climbed the steps of the verandah, then she'd shyly give in and allow the old man to get his seventy-year-old-arms around her, but not for long. Grandpappy would only have enough energy left to give her a loving peck on the cheek before he would turn for his white rocking chair lest he keel over right there on the spot. And that's exactly what he did do one day. Poor Anna. She blamed herself for not having had enough sense to recognize his frail condition. Anna must have cared for the old man a great deal because right after his death, she slipped into a great despair and simply left the plantation one morning without saying a word. I never saw Anna again, and she didn't get to hear the reading of my grandpappy's will, so I suppose her inheritance is still sitting in a bank account in New Orleans drawing interest.*

*I idolized the old man. I'd learned so much from my grandpappy, having spent the winter school months with him at his plantation and his house in New Orleans throughout most of my childhood. Grandpa-*

*ppy always said having me around made him feel young again. And he certainly took pleasure in teaching me all he knew about business.*

*But it was sailing on his yacht to Jamaica and the other islands of the Carribean that thrilled me the most. Grandpappy taught me at an early age the difference between work and play, and he also taught me how to put the two of them together to make money. Of course, play included practical jokes along with the fine art of pleasuring women.*

*The old man made certain I realized I was living a life quite out of the ordinary, far different from the lives most people lived. Sailing the Carribean with my Grandpappy and roaming the streets of the French Quarter in New Orleans by myself seemed only natural, and I often felt different from my childhood friends. The ways and language of the streets of New Orleans, and of the islands, was far from offensive to my mind, and an education in itself.*

*But it was the travel that had me hook, line and sinker. I lusted for other islands far away. Islands I had only heard tales of from sailors and drunks when grandpappy and I would reach a new port, or sit in one of those old, broken-down bars Grandpappy loved in Haiti or Havana. Grandpappy was determined I would get an education equal to one provided by any university in the world, but a much more practical one.*

In Mexia, Texas during the throws of the oil boom, Ernest's father managed to drill six wells, all of which were dry. In the process, while the family was going broke, Ernest's mother decided to use the few remaining dollars she and her husband had to set-up a dormitory style structure for the wildcatters. In this atmosphere, she went into the catering business, and Ernest was always at her side in the kitchen. It was his mother who instructed and encouraged him in the fine art of culinary skills and a love of spices. At four-years-old, he would stand on a stool and stir the family meals in her large pots and pans over a wood-burning stove. How could anyone have known of the adventures that lay ahead for this young lad from

Cajun country in Louisiana, some of them spine tingling and life threatening while others would be just plain mischievous and full of skulduggery.

# Hot Tail Feathers

The first of these adventures occurred on a hot, humid August afternoon when Ernest was invited to visit with a cousin in a nearby township. The fun started when his cousin caught an unsuspecting buzzard. Like all young boys, mischief seemed to come first. But not always as evil as what these two had in mind. Ernest's cousin, Jim, held the critter while Ernest tied its feet with a bandanna soaked in kerosene. Pulling a match from his pocket, Ernest lit the rag.

*The buzzard panicked and became frantic in an attempt to escape the flames. Cousin Jim turned the buzzard free by tossing it into the air, and Jim and I stood by and watched the beleaguered bird fly away. It circled overhead before it unpredictably landed on my uncle's barn roof. The damn bird just sat there frantically struggling with the burning rag. Finally, it picked itself free, and when we last saw it, the buzzard was flying south to cool its injured tail feathers. Although the two of us were thoroughly entertained and amused by what we had just witnessed, we completely forget about the burning bandanna, which still lay atop the barn's roof. It was only a matter of minutes before the building was fully engulfed in a nice warm afternoon blaze, and not much longer before it burnt to the ground.*

While at work with his mother in her kitchen to cook up grub for the wildcatters, Ernest began to spend some of his free time with his father on the oilrigs in an attempt to learn the oil business. It was then when seven became his lucky number.

*Late one October afternoon while clearing up for the day the seventh well, a genuine gusher, came in.*

By this time, his mother wanted him to think about going to a university, but Ernest had other ideas. He took the savings he earned in her kitchen, and his share from the oil strike, and went around the world, twice. It took more than two years. He traveled to such places as Hawai`i, Tahiti, Borneo, Brunei, Singapore, Japan, Hong Kong and China, across India and Africa then to the islands of the Caribbean and on to Central and South America before he returned to what had become his beloved South Seas Island paradise.

Although he eventually returned home to Mexia, he had decided he was going to enjoy life, his way, and on his own terms.

*Since then, I've had a fun and rewarding life, have never received a paycheck, and have lived solely by my wits. Survival has been fun. My number-one rule quickly became: Enjoy life and spend every penny I make.*

People have estimated the personal wealth Ernest, a.k.a. Don the Beachcomber, spent in this endeavor ranged upwards to over thirty million dollars. Of the trip, Don the Beachcomber said, *I always considered the two-year trip around the world an adventure and education unequaled by anything any college could have offered. I saw the elephants and I heard the owls.*

# Okolehau and a Wahine

It was early morning, August 21, 1929, when at the age of twenty-two Ernest finally breathed a sigh of relief. After a six-day cruise out of San Pedro filled with storms and high seas, his one hundred-twenty foot yacht had come upon the welcome beacon of Diamond Head Lighthouse. This was the first trip to Hawai`i for several members of the crew. As for Ernest, he had been there twice before. Once in 1925, and again in 1927. But, the sight of the beacon meant he had finally returned.

*For everyone's benefit, the Captain took a leisurely course to the southwest so the crew could take in the beauty of Oahu, and the lovely cloud covered, mist enshrouded Ko'olau Mountains. As the island drew nearer and the sun rose to our backs, we could see the breathtaking aqua-green shallows just beyond the reef. Rounding Diamond Head Crater, we sailed quite close to shore towards the port of Honolulu. It was at this very spot only four years before when, for the first time, I experienced the fragrance and aromas of the pungent earthy scent of the tropics. It was like a wet blanket soaked in a floral perfume.*

Don the Beachcomber at Waikiki Beach with Diamond Head
in background

Hawai`i was just as he remembered, and he often remarked, *The scene always comes back to me in living color any time I smell frangipani, tuberose or ginger.*

After they docked at pier six, the crew immediately went to work to tidy up before they disappeared along the waterfront. Ernest wouldn't need them for a couple of days, and he wanted to look around himself and track down the supplies he needed.

He wandered around Honolulu and eventually drifted to the beach in front of the Moana Hotel where he bumped into a fellow by the name of Duke Kahanamoku. Duke was a handsome lad, an Olympic gold and silver medalist in swimming, and an accomplished surfer. Over the next few days, Ernest had a marvelous stay in Honolulu, and he spent as much time on Waikiki Beach as possible. One afternoon Ernest and his new friend, Duke, got a small boat and rowed out to meet a ship arriving from California. With leis draped over their arms and around their necks, they climbed onboard. Dressed in swimming attire they met and greeted the new visitors to the islands, and Ernest learned the meaning of Aloha. Duke and Ernest remained close friends throughout their lives.

Ernest Gantt and Duke Kahanamoku

After several happy, fun-filled days ashore, it was finally time to return to the yacht and set sail, but when he arrived back at the pier, he found the crew, along with the captain, hadn't shown up.

*With the help of several off-duty members of the Honolulu police force Duke introduced me to, I finally succeeded in chasing down the errant crew who had been severely watered down with okolehau, a local alco-*

*holic concoction. It wasn't of any help, either, that some damn wahines had tried to persuade them to overstay their visas.*

Ernest dragged the reluctant crew back to the pier, but this was not one of his most pleasant experiences. Still, once on board the yacht, the men fell in line and were on their way across the South Pacific.

Three weeks later the group arrived in Tahiti several days ahead of schedule. Once again, the crew disappeared the moment their work was completed. Ernest said he didn't blame them. His last visit to Tahiti in 1927 was most memorable, and he left the yacht as soon as he possibly could. During his stay ashore when he wasn't chasing down supplies, he visited old friends and learned more about this most colorful south seas paradise. Nor had Ernest forgotten about the beautiful Tahitian maidens, ... *many of whom walked the beaches almost completely in the buff. For some reason, this time there seemed to be more of them than before. They seemed to be all over the place.*

It was during this visit to Tahiti while he was in the company of one of those beautiful maidens when he was introduced to an old Tahitian woman who called him 'Marama' which she said meant 'The Far Seeing.'

Needless to say, the very same crew problems that occurred in Honolulu repeated themselves in Tahiti. Ready to set sail, he assured his Tahitian family he would return. Ernest enlisted the assistance of the local gendarmes, and the rescue of the crew was accomplished with dispatch.

*It was very hard in those days to hide twenty-four light-skinned new-comers in Tahiti,* Don the Beachcomber said years later. *But one of them did manage to avoid my rescue attempts, and I have always insisted he was highjacked by some damn wahine, and is still living in those lovely, lovely islands of French Polynesia with many grandchildren.*

Departure from Papeete wasn't at all easy this time around because Ernest felt like destiny had brought him back for some reason. But, leave he did, and three and a half weeks later he arrived in Sydney, Australia only two days late.

In order to be a part of the crew on the cruise, Ernest's father had agreed to be responsible for his son's actions so Ernest could hire on as the Supercargo of his uncle's new yacht. The crew was to deliver the beautiful creation to his uncle upon his arrival in Sydney from Galveston, Texas via London. In short order a worried Ernest Gantt found his employer and explained the reasons for the delay. To Ernest's relief, the man simply laughed and seemed to understand completely.

After a few days seeing the sights in Sydney, Ernest was on his way for a one-year journey as a merchant seaman aboard various freighters through the ports of the South Seas.

*I had the time of my life in such exotic places as Port Moresby in Indonesia, Papua New Guinea, Fiji, Tonga, Rarotonga in the Cook Islands, Papeete in Tahiti, and Honolulu before ending up in Hollywood where I began a new life.*

# *Hollywood*

Life took Ernest Raymond Beaumont Gantt through many phases, and the beaches he combed were far and wide.

In 1931 at age twenty-four, he arrived in Hollywood at the start of the depression and the depths of prohibition. But, he was determined to make a name for himself. Was Ernest simply another star-struck young man, eager for the spotlight? Possibly. But if so, life quickly took him along a different path.

Exhausted of funds after another year of adventure, he found the easiest path to food was in the soup kitchens of Chinatown. It was here where he took advantage of the situation and supplemented his knowledge of the delights of Chinese food dishes. He also polished his mastery and dexterity in the use of chopsticks, a skill first developed while visiting China, and a skill he later used while teaching many of Hollywood's biggest stars.

Like other out-of-work men, Ernest took odd jobs wherever he could. At one time he parked cars, and other times he bootlegged whisky to make ends meet.

It was during this period when he often ate dinner at Simon's Cafeteria for twenty-five cents. Here he came across and made friends with the likes of David Niven, Marlene Dietrich, Clark Gable and Tubby Brocolli. With the connections he made in the movie industry, Ernest became a technical advisor on several South Seas productions including 'Moon of Manakura' and 'Hell's Half Acre.'

Money may have been in short supply, but the one thing Ernest always had was an abundance of dreams, along with his South Seas expertise, props, spears, shells and any manner of whatnots.

Ernest Gantt and entrance to Don's Beachcomber Bar and Restaurant

By December 5, 1933, Ernest thought he had more than a clue as to the way a bar and restaurant business should be operated. On a little side street just off Hollywood Boulevard he discovered a 'For Rent' sign on a tailor shop that had gone broke. He rented the space connected to the McCadden Hotel for thirty dollars a month with a five-year lease. The space was thirteen by thirty feet. As he had very little money, he acquired the lease with his word and a handshake. Here he set up a bar with stools, which accommodated thirty people, and five small tables with chairs. Ernest decorated the place with his collection of South Seas artifacts, some flotsam of old nets and parts of ships he had found along the San Pedro waterfront. At the suggestion of friends who had often called him Don because of his bootlegging days, Ernest created a handcrafted driftwood sign and hung it out front. The sign read—*Don's Beachcomber.* Two Philippine boys served the tables and two more assisted him behind the bar.

Ernest Gantt behind the bar at McCadden Street Don's
Beachcomber

In the words of Don the Beachcomber, *With prohibition officially repealed, and recognizing that people hadn't tasted a decent drink during the previous fourteen years of darkness, with the smell of Rhum always in my nostrils, I started to concoct some unusual, and at the time, exotic drinks.*

The first of these was the Sumatra Kula which originally sold for twenty-five cents. Other drinks with tropical sounding names were soon to follow and were listed on the mirror behind the bar. Among these, all made with thirty year old rhum were, the Sumatra Kula, the fourteen-ounce Zombie, which sold for one dollar and seventy-five cents, the Mai Tai Swizzle, Beachcomber's Gold, Missionary's

Downfall, Cuban Daiquiri, the Pearl Diver and Don's Pearl. A genuine pearl was placed into every fifth Don's Pearl. In the Zombie, Ernest used five different rhums, one of which was a hundred-fifty proof.

Eventually the bar and restaurant became known as Don the Beachcomber, and through the years, Ernest—Don the Beachcomber—hosted over 23,000,000 dinner guests. The promise he made to his customers: *I always told my guests: If you can't get to paradise, I'll bring it to you. And, I did.*

# The Zombie

The most lethal tropical drink ever created was the original Zombie, which Don the Beachcomber mixed as a special drink for a friend.

*Late one afternoon Jack came into the Don's Beachcomber just off Hollywood Boulevard and ordered 'a tall cool one' before his flight to San Francisco. The original Zombie was a real man-killer.*

During his early years in Jamaica, Ernest learned all he could about the spirit derived from sugarcane.

*What all good bar tenders throughout the Caribbean knew, when several varieties of rhum are mixed together the effects of each are intensified.*

With the Zombie, he used this knowledge to his advantage. He mixed tropical rhum concoctions with more than one variety of rhum, and created many exotic recipes. For this man-killer he mixed a concoction of five different rums, along with other ingredients that were not only pleasant to look at, but were tasty and went down smoothly.

After he enjoyed the first Zombie served anywhere in the world, Ernest's friend, Jack, finished two more before he left the new McCadden Street establishment. Several days later he returned and wanted to know what was in the drink. It seems upon leaving Don's Beachcomber after the three drinks, he had a fight with his chauffeur, got into an argument on the airplane, and later found himself seated on the docks in San Francisco with his feet dangling in the water.

*Jack said he pinched himself but felt nothing. I said to him, You were like the walking dead.*

From that day on the mixture was called the Zombie and Ernest's customers were limited to only two of these drinks because of their potency.

On another occasion, a very well dressed, handsome gentleman came into Ernest's domain. He seated himself at the bar and ordered two Zombies. When he asked for a third, he was told by the bartender the house rules permitted only two. When he heard this, the fellow asked to see the manager.

After Ernest re-explained the house rules, the fellow insisted, *I'll bet one hundred dollars I can handle at least five of the blasted things without any problem whatsoever.*

Ernest immediately suggested that since he had already had the limit that he come back another day. *I said I would match his one hundred dollar wager with one hundred dollars of my own, and bet he couldn't finish three.*

A few days later the neatly dressed gentleman who Ernest had previously recognized as a member of the local mob, arrived with a couple of friends. He handed over a one hundred dollar bill for the bartender to hold, and Ernest matched the wager.

*Two Zombies were sat in front of the gentleman, and he drank both them down. Halfway through the third Zombie the fellow's head hit the counter top.*

Ernest took the two hundred dollars held by the bartender and warned the man's stunned companions, *Always remember The Beachcomber's Rule number two. Never bet on another man's game.*

No one knew Ernest had laced the Zombies with glycerin in order to make them go down more smoothly, and enter the blood system faster than usual.

# Marlene Dietrich

A few days after the grand opening of Don's Beachcomber, another distinguished looking gentleman dropped in and ordered a *Sumatra Kula* from the bar list. When he finished the drink he said, *It was the first really good drink I've had for a donkey's year,* and ordered another one. After the third one he introduced himself as Neil Vanderbilt, a roving reporter for the New York Tribune, and he promised to bring his friends to sample some of Ernest's rhum drinks. A few days later Mr. Vanderbilt arrived with Charlie Chaplin and three other men. Asked to suggest the best drinks, Ernest served up five of his newly created concoctions. Three rounds later, all of them departed in a happy state.

Neil Vanderbilt and Ernest Gantt

After Ernest opened what he often called *"my little establishment in Hollywood"* in 1933, he became a serious inventor of exotic tropical rum concoctions. These included the Mai Tai—originally called the Mai Tai Swizzle—the Zombie, Missionary's Downfall and the Beachcomber's Daiquiri to name a few. Each drink was created for a mood, climate, or time of day. For example: the Zombie and the Cuban Daiquiri were created for afternoon sipping, while the Beachcomber's Gold and Beachcomber's Daiquiri were for early evening around sundown, the Mai Tai and the Pi Yi were for later.

During the following days Ernest's tiny *Don's Beachcomber* bar and restaurant grew to be filled to over-flow capacity with motion pictures stars, directors and producers, all of whom had heard about the place thanks to Mr. Vanderbilt. Here the stars of the stage and silver screen could have good drinks, and most important of all, there were no autograph hunters around because Ernest would not allow autograph seekers in, and cameras were not allowed.

The list of stars, many of whom Ernest developed close, personal relationships with, ran the gambit from Charlie Chaplin, The Marx Brothers and Rudy Vallee to Garbo, Clark Gable, Bing Crosby, Mae West and others.

Donn Beach often told the following story about Marlene Dietrich.

*Just after eleven o'clock one evening after the completion of a film, Marlene arrived with over a dozen friends. People were already jammed around my little bar watching the original drunken Mynah Bird 'Rajah' eat whisky soaked pieces of apple, only to eventually fall of his perch and stumble around while trying to walk along the bar. I had trained Rajah to say, 'Give me a beer. Give me a beer. Give me a beer, stupid!'*

*This time, Marlene took one of the empty stools I had reserved for her and her director. She watched intently while I began to mix what became her favorite drink, the 'Beachcomber's Gold,' in which I used thirty year old Jamaican rhum. When finished, the drink was poured over shaved ice tossed into a champagne glass and formed into the shape of a fan. The Beachcomber's Gold was simply exquisite according to Marlene. When I handed Marlene her drink, someone bumped her and the iced cold contents of the cold glass spilled down the plunging neckline of her elegant gold lame gown.*

*There was no toilet in Don's Beachcomber. My customers had to go outside, through the hotel lobby, up a flight of stairs and down a hallway to get to one. And the restroom wasn't of proper size or a real ladies room. I quickly grabbed a towel and Marlene's arm and whisked her out of the bar and into the Ladies Lounge. With the door open, I sat her down and handed her the towel, and then turned to close the door to leave.*

'For Christ's sake help me,' she yelled. 'I can't get my gown off.'

Standing in the wide open doorway and feeling like an idiot, I began to gently pull her gown off her shoulders when she suddenly grabbed the straps from my hands and yanked the top down to her waist. She didn't turn red-faced, but simply looked at me and said, 'Don, dry me off, quickly.'

I took the bar towel from her lap and started very gingerly to dry each of her beautifully, pearl shaped breasts. When she looked up and saw my face she began to laugh, and said, 'Don, you look like you've just seen a ghost.'"

I have, I thought to myself. And never a lovelier pair at that.

Marlene always received pleasure in telling the story whenever the chance permitted. This she did with delight just to see the look it brought to my face.

# Gone to the Islands

By now most of Ernest's customers called him, Don, taking the lead from the *Don's Beachcomber* sign out front of his little bar. The name *Don* actually came from his rum-running, bootlegging days with Tony Canero, a Los Angeles mobster, who often referred to him as a *Don*.

To increase business late at night Don would often go outside and turn on a garden hose, which he had affixed above the bar's corrugated metal roof. This created the illusion of rain, and just enough of a reason for patrons to remain for another round or two of drinks.

Once when he went on vacation to Honolulu, he sent out the following notice to his customers: *To us Beachcombers, Spring means Fishing and Housecleaning. For two to four weeks commencing April 27, we will be doing both. During this period our place will be closed and Don will be on his plantation in Hawai`i selecting coconuts and pineapples that have been missing from our tables these past four years. Please give me a call about May 15 at HO-3968.* On the back of the mail-out was the following: *Don the Beachcomber has compiled a partial list of outstanding restaurants in Los Angeles and vicinity for your convenience.* The list included the names of seventeen restaurants along with their phone numbers.

# IT'S SPRING

*To some folks Spring means "a young
man's fancy, etc.," or buds bursting on the
trees, or song writers and poets.*

To us BEACHCOMBERS, Spring
means Fishing and Housecleaning.
For two to four weeks
commencing April 27, we will be
doing both. During this
period our place will be closed
and DON will be on his
plantation in Hawaii selecting
the coconuts and pineapples
that have been missing from our
tables these past four years.

PLEASE GIVE US A CALL ABOUT MAY 15, AT HO-3968

Notice to Customers

In the earlier days when he was still near broke, Don kept the day's cash receipts with him in a cigar box while he slept under the bar. When he wanted to get away to his favorite haunt, Honolulu, he put the cash box under his arm, locked the doors and hung a sign outside that read: *Gone to the Islands.*

Because of his contacts, the unique and dimly lighted Polynesian atmosphere and the exotic rhum concoctions, *Don's Beachcomber* was extremely popular with over ninety percent of the reservations being held by movie stars.

*I went to extreme lengths in order to preserve the secrets of my drink recipes,* Don said. *From the beginning I realized rivals would try to raid my establishment of employees in an effort to copy the formulae. First, I removed the labels from all bottles and used a method of codes so employ-ees could not memorize the various ingredients and proportions of my concoctions. Numbers and letters were placed on the bottles. Recipes were written in code for the bartenders, all trained by me, to follow.*

Because of how rowdy his customers became, complaints from neighbors in the local community caused the California Equalization Board to require his saloon to serve food as well as liquor. It was only a very short time before they fully realized what their actions did for *Don's Beachcomber.*

*My little saloon/restaurant with its wonderful drinks and cuisine pre-sentations became so successful that two years later in 1935 it grossed over five hundred dollars a day. One hundred from the food, and four hundred profit.*

In 1937 a new and larger location had to be leased across the street from the original site. This new location had enough space for a bar and restaurant seating one hundred seventy-five guests. The name above the entrance now read, *Don the Beachcomber.* Inside the entrance on a pillar in a glass case were ornamental bamboo tubes used to encase the personalized chop sticks of many of Hollywood's famous with their names burnt into the surface of their individual tube.

Even though the popularity of the restaurant grew, it was com-mon practice for customers to be turned away even when the place wasn't full.

*At times a customer would arrive at the front door only to find a vel-vet rope stretched across the entryway. This only served to whet the cus-tomer's appetite for what was inside.*

And to get in, one had to be properly dressed, and remain prop-erly dressed while on the premises.

*One evening Orson Wells removed his jacket. When asked to put it back on he announced that he 'would never again visit such a stuffy place.' And he never did, either, until the following week.*

By 1938 Don had spent more than $7,800.00 for fresh leis of gardenias and other expensive flowers he wore every day. These were flown in from Hawai`i on Pan Am Clipper planes.

He would also sell flower leis and other Polynesian items from an alcove just off the hallway entrance of his restaurant. This idea was the forerunner of souvenir shops in connection with some of the more famous and popular restaurants of today. At midnight every night he presented the prettiest girl in the place with a gardenia lei.

By 1939 copies of the Don the Beachcomber Polynesian style bar and restaurant began to pop up around the country, with fifteen in the Los Angeles area alone.

*I had to file a lawsuit against one outfit in New York, Monte Poser's Beachcomber Restaurant, for using the Beachcomber name,* Don said. *With Lillian Gish and Alfred Hitchcock as witnesses, and after four months of legal sparing, a consent decree was issued against these plagiarizes by Federal Judge Cramer and complied with. Not only were Poser and others restrained from using the Beachcomber name, they were also not allowed to sell the Zombie or any other of my famous rhum concoctions. The consent decree also barred Poser from using menus, or any formulae, recipe, method of preparation or service of foods or concoctions I originated. The operator of the restaurant was even in the habit of telling his guests to 'visit our original the next time you're in Los Angeles.' Also named in the consent decree was the Missionaries Downfall, Pi Yi, Coconut Rhum and Kona Coffee Grog as well as sixty-three more of my original concoctions.*

Another copycat, the most famous of all, was Trader Vic's, owned and operated by Vic Bergeron whom Don helped start up in business in Oakland, California.

*Vic's business wasn't affected by this court decision because of the friendship between the two of us. Vic had purchased over eight thousand dollars worth of authentic Polynesian items of decor from me to start up his operation. I also loaned him several of my employees in order for the first Trader Vic Restaurant to be opened on time, and I have always complimented Vic as my greatest imitator.*

In one way, Don didn't really mind the reckless abandon with which these copycats sprang up, for not a one of them knew anything about The Trade Winds Trading Company. This company, which Don owned, was the supplier of all the bamboo, mattings and other Polynesian artifacts and materials the copycats needed, and had to purchase in order to furnish their look-a-like bars and eateries. Don was also certain not one of them could offer the same combination of quality food, service and drinks he did.

*I often explained away the popularity of my Polynesian Paradise by saying, We are all escapists at heart.*

The Don the Beachcomber Restaurants and Don's escape to Polynesia philosophy influenced many people. Not only did they come to visit his restaurants to indulge in items to please the palate, some of them became collectors of rhum and Polynesian memorabilia from his establishments, and from copycats all across the country.

Jack Thorpe, a very successful businessman from Grosse Pointe Woods, Michigan became one of the most serious collectors of rhum from all over the world. Jack would travel from one restaurant to another and knew most of Don the Beachcomber employees by first name.

*I befriended Jack, and always looked upon him with great fondness. One bottle Jack never opened was his most prized possessions, a bottle of 1907, thirty year old Meyers (V.V.O.) Rum labeled as Fine Jamaican Rum, Bottled in Jamaica. Jack was presented this as a gift from a glass showcase by my good friend, Meyers attorney, G. A. Dunkley, who was the Director of Meyers Rum in Nassua, Bahama.*

# Don's Polynesian Island Plantation

Because of the virtual monopoly on Polynesian furnishings and artifacts Don the Beachcomber had, he set up a special fund. With the money, he eventually built his Polynesian Plantation in Encino, California next door to his good friend, Clark Gable. The Plantation became a gorgeous re-creation of a real South Seas paradise completely furnished with the curios he had collected for himself over the years. Here among the Pandanus covered huts and lily filled pools and springs were Gala and Pagos, the three hundred pound Galapagos Turtles. These creatures lived at the Plantation, and constantly provided entertainment at the private luaus he held for his friends and other Hollywood stars who enjoyed the Polynesian lifestyle.

Galapagos Turtle at Encino Plantation

The grounds of his Plantation were completely landscaped throughout with thatched huts. A thatched longhouse was surrounded by tropical plants, palm trees and a banana grove. The lily filled pools and waterfalls added flavor and made the Plantation a Polynesian tropical paradise showplace, and Don was more popular than before. Here he built a replica of a treehouse he had seen during his travels in Papua New Guinea. He also created an evening downpour, but this time he added thunder, fog and lightening. In order to make his Plantation even more authentic, Don even went so far as to purchase a ten-acre parcel of land in Kailua on the island of Oahu in Hawai`i. He stripped the coconuts from the trees, shipped them to Hollywood, and then attached them with wires to the palm trees at his Plantation. Only Walter Houston recognized the wrong fruit was on the wrong tree.

Movie stars at Encino Plantation luau

Ambience around pool for Encino luau

The menu for his Plantation feasts included salted roasted Kukui nuts (inamona), opihi and limu (opihu a me limu), dried squid with red salt (paakai ulaula), dried aku (aku koala), steamed crabs (papa'i mahu ia), mullet packed in ti leaves (lawalu amaama), kalua pig (kalua puaa), baked sweet potatoes (uala maola hoomo'a), poi, chicken and luau in coconut milk (mo, luau, a ma wai niu), limi salmon (kamamo lomi), bananas (maia), coconut pudding (haupia), fresh pineapple (hala kahiki), and manoa fruit punch, along with his exotic rhum concoctions.

The roasted pig at luau

Many of the special effects installed at his tropical paradise in Encino were completed with help of some of Hollywood's best special effects technicians of the day. With a throw of a switch, rain and thunder would be induced in the late evening, not to keep paying customers around a little longer, *but to keep the girls from leaving the special parties arranged for my movie star friends.*

The many exciting experiences of Don the Beachcomber's early life helped him to develop an air of sophistication, which in many ways resembled a combination of two of his closest friends, Douglas Fairbanks Sr. and Clark Gable. But he also had a mischievous streak similar to that of another friend, Error Flynn. When he realized what was happening to him, Don made every effort to keep the image alive. For example, during his days as Major Don Beach-Comber in the Mediterranean Theater of Operations during World War II, he had all of his military uniforms especially tailored-made at the best shops in London.

# A Giant Sawfish

During this era when the motion picture industry was making real headway into the entertainment hearts of millions of Americans and people worldwide, *Selected Shorts,* as they were called, were presented before any feature length film. Don joined up with his friend and filmmaker, Swansey Austin, for an expedition to the mouth of the Yakki River around Mazatlan in Mexico to produce a film on Sawfish. They knew little of what lay ahead, but hearing what they considered exaggerated stories, the two of them loaded up a Ford Station Wagon with fishing gear, harpoons, pith helmets and expectations. With a variety of his favorite rhums and selected bourbons in hand, the two men drove six days along some of the most horrible roads either of them had ever seen into the interior of Central America to the mouth of the Yakki River. Arriving on location, they hired several extras from the local populace and proceeded to set up camp for the start of filming the next day. By the end of the evening both men were quite exhausted when they finally settled down for a good sleep. Around midnight they were surprised to be awakened with swarms of minute black insects called Hahines covering their bodies. In Tahiti they are called Nonos. Americans know them as gnats. These Hahines feasted on the available fresh human flesh the two new white men had brought into the territory, and left their proboscis buried deep in the soft skin.

A hooked 2,000 pound Sawfish in Mexico

The success Don and Swansey had in filming the *Short* was beyond their wildest dreams. Although fraught with danger, Don had the time of his life. But pity the poor Sawfish. Standing in the bow of a canoe, the first off-balance throw Don made with the harpoon hit a glancing blow to the head, while the second harpoon scored a hit with pin point accuracy right in the tail section. The twenty-seven foot Sawfish, now tethered by a rope to the canoe, was no more that ten feet away when the attack began. It jumped and stirred up the water creating such a turbulence in the lagoon that Don was toppled right out of the canoe and into the muddy water. Juan, the local fellow who was paddling, and Swansey, who was in another canoe doing the filming, helped Don back on board, but not before a few panic-filled moments.

*I collected my wits,* Don later said of the incident, *and picked up another harpoon and sent it flying through the heart. A direct hit.*

The men quickly attached another rope to the monster, which weighed more than two thousand pounds, and hauled it closer to shore where their local helpers had attached a heavy-duty pulley to the low hanging branches of a tree. When the creature was hoisted from the lagoon, the crew of eleven men watched while it gave birth to more than a dozen live babies, each about fifteen inches long.

Baby Sawfish

Before they could return to Hollywood, Don and Swansey spent several days at rest, and they drank up most of their supply of rhum and bourbon in a desperate attempt to recuperate from the swelling that had occurred on their arms and legs as a result of the bites of the Hahines. Finally, they loaded up the Ford Station Wagon with their gear and a tank, which held four of the baby Sawfish. Then, they headed back for Hollywood and the Warner Brothers Studios. When Mrs. Jack Warner, an avowed environmentalist, heard of the episode and saw the live babies on display at the Warner Brothers Studio, she hit the roof and put the kibosh on everything.

*Although the film was never released, I can tell you I had a wonderful time catching a twenty-two foot Sawfish weighing more than 2,000 pounds.*

# *Havanas*

Over the years Don the Beachcomber searched the Caribbean and West Indies for the finest rhums available. In this part of the world, he developed close friendships with Oswald Henriques of J. Wray & Nephew Ltd., and Fred Meyers, owner of Meyers Rhum in Jamaica. At one point in time, he was told his interest in the growing of sugarcane and the distilling process was unique among American businessman. Don's awareness of the importance of accurate chemical control of the rhum distilling process and the actual taste of the rhum became so acute that several of his thoughts and ideas where incorporated in the manufacture of the product by the various rhum producers. On visits to Jamaica and Cuba spanning a number of years, Don the Beachcomber spent many days walking the sugarcane fields to study the processing procedures at the distillation plants. Several rhums were specially blended under his direction so they would be adaptable and suitable for mixing with various tropical fruits.

Ernest Gantt at J. Way in Jamaica

Ernest in sugarcane field and at J. Wray laboratory

Over time, he developed the habit of making buying trips where he would purchase a two-year supply of rhum for his establishments. Backed by many years of experience as a traveler and student of rhums of the West Indies such as Cuba, Porto Rico, Jamaica, Haiti, Trinidad and Barbadoes, Don tried rhum after rhum, and various combinations of rhums and he skillfully blended them with spices and tropical fruit juices until a perfectly balanced rhum drink was developed. In 1939 in Jamaica, the title of Ambassador of Rhum was officially bestowed upon him by leaders of the rhum industry. By

1945 he was the largest single user of the beverage worldwide, serving over 325,000 cases.

Unique to his Don the Beachcomber restaurants, which didn't have a wine list or a wine cellar, his rhum menus listed his full stock of one hundred thirty-eight brands of rhum stored in his rhum cellar. These rhums came from sixteen different countries, and the menu listed sixty of his original tropical rhum concoctions.

*I have always claimed that Rhum holds certain therapeutic values and is the purest spirit made, the greatest of all drinks because it is distilled from sugar cane, and is easily assimilated into the body's system.*

## FINE RUMS FROM DON THE BEACHCOMBER'S CELLAR

### CUBA

| | | |
|---|---|---|
| Alvarez Carta Camp Gold | Cuba $ | .40 |
| Alvarez Carta Camp Matusalem (15 years old) | Cuba | .50 |
| Alvarez Carta Camp Silver | Cuba | .40 |
| Anejo | Cuba | .45 |
| Bacardi Elixir | Cuba | .60 |
| Bacardi 1873 | Cuba | .60 |
| Bacardi Carta de Oro | Cuba | .40 |
| Bacardi Carta Blanca | Cuba | .40 |
| Beachcomber's (6 years old) | Cuba | .40 |
| Bebida | Cuba | .40 |
| Bellow's Malecon Gold | Cuba | .40 |
| Bellow's Malecon Silver | Cuba | .40 |
| Bolero | Cuba | .40 |
| Caballero | Cuba | .45 |
| Cubanola (12 years old) | Cuba | .60 |
| Daiquiri | Cuba | .45 |
| Havana Club | Cuba | .40 |
| Palau (30 years old) | Cuba | .60 |
| Ron Albuerne | Cuba | .40 |
| Ron Caney | Cuba | .40 |
| Ron el Infierno (20 years old) | Cuba | .45 |
| Ron Superior Farnon | Cuba | .40 |
| Royal Scarlet Carta D'oro | Cuba | .40 |
| Sloppy Joe's Rum | Cuba | .40 |
| Tango Superior | Cuba | .40 |

### DEMERARA

| | | |
|---|---|---|
| Booker's Liqueur | Demerara | .45 |
| Don's Private Brand 150 Proof | Demerara | .60 |
| Ellis' Demerara 142 Proof | British Guiana | .45 |
| Hedges & Butler | Demerara | .50 |
| Hudson's Bay Demerara 91 Proof | British Guiana | .45 |
| Hudson's Bay Demerara 151 Proof | British Guiana | .60 |
| Lamb's Old Navy | British West Indies | .45 |
| Lemon Hart 96 Proof | Demerara | .45 |
| Lemon Hart 114 Proof | British Guiana | .60 |
| Lemon Hart 151 Proof | British Guiana | .60 |
| Lownde's (Don's Private Label) 96 Proof | Demerara | .45 |
| (Blended Specially for Don the Beachcomber) | | |
| Lownde's (Don's Private Label) 151 Proof | Demerara | .60 |
| Southard's Western Pearl | Demerara | .45 |
| Trower's Gold Lion 100 Proof | Demerara | .45 |
| Trower's Gold Lion 151 Proof | Demerara | .60 |

### MARTINIQUE

| | | |
|---|---|---|
| Alexis Godillot | Martinique | .45 |
| Barum | Martinique | .45 |
| Black Head Grog | Martinique | .40 |
| Black Head Punch | Martinique | .40 |
| Black Head Rum | Martinique | .40 |
| Colonial Divina | Martinique | .45 |
| Don's Private Brand | Martinique | .45 |
| Rhum Charleston | Martinique | .45 |
| Risetta | Martinique | .45 |
| Usine Sainte Marie | Martinique | .45 |

### JAMAICA

| | | |
|---|---|---|
| Ballantine | Jamaica $ | .45 |
| Bellow's Choicest Liqueur | Jamaica | .60 |
| Bellow's Finest Liqueur | Jamaica | .45 |
| Burke's (6 years old) | Jamaica | .45 |
| Charley's Red Label | Jamaica | .45 |
| Charley's Royal Reserve (15 years old) | Jamaica | .50 |
| Don's Private Brand | Jamaica | .45 |
| Ellis 148 Proof | Jamaica | .75 |
| Finzi's Ruby | Jamaica | .45 |
| Fulcher's | Jamaica | .45 |
| Gilbey's Governor General | Jamaica | .45 |
| Grange Hill | Jamaica | .45 |
| Hedges & Butler | Jamaica | .50 |
| Hudson's Bay 91 | Jamaica | .45 |
| Hudson's Bay 151 Proof | Jamaica | .60 |
| Kelly's Gold Seal | Jamaica | .50 |
| Kelly's Grande Reserve | Jamaica | .60 |
| Kelly's Punch Rum | Jamaica | .40 |
| Kelly's White Label | Jamaica | .45 |
| Lamb's Golden Grove | Jamaica | .45 |
| Lemon Hart Twenty-eight Years | Jamaica | 1.00 |
| Lemon Hart Planter's | Jamaica | .45 |
| Lemon Hart Liqueur | Jamaica | .60 |
| Lemon Hart V.O. | Jamaica | .45 |
| Lownde's (Don's Private Label) | Jamaica | .45 |
| Myer's Light Vatted | Jamaica | .45 |
| Myer's Mona (30 years old) | Jamaica | .80 |
| Myer's Planter's Punch (8 years old) | Jamaica | .45 |
| Myer's V.O. (13 years old) | Jamaica | .75 |
| Pirate Brand | Jamaica | .45 |
| Southard's Old London Dock | Jamaica | .45 |
| St. James, Des Plantation | Jamaica | .60 |
| Sugar Loaf | Jamaica | .60 |
| Treasure Cove (32 years old) | Jamaica | 1.25 |
| (Oldest and Finest Jamaica Rum in the World— Natural Strength—74 Proof) | | |
| Trower's | Jamaica | .40 |
| White's Red Heart | Jamaica | .45 |
| J. Wray & Nephew's Dagger Punch | Jamaica | .45 |
| J. Wray & Nephew's Green Label | Jamaica | .40 |
| J. Wray & Nephew's Golden Stag (6 years old) | Jamaica | .45 |
| J. Wray & Nephew's† (5 years old) | Jamaica | .40 |
| J. Wray & Nephew's†† (7 years old) | Jamaica | .45 |
| J. Wray & Nephew's††† (10 years old) | Jamaica | .50 |
| J. Wray & Nephew's Special Reserve (17 years old) | Jamaica | .60 |
| (Bottled Exclusively for Don the Beachcomber) | | |

### PANAMA

| | | |
|---|---|---|
| Beachcomber's (4 years old) | Panama | .40 |
| Gorgona | Panama | .45 |

### DUTCH EAST INDIES

| | | |
|---|---|---|
| Batavia Arak | Batavia | .75 |

### VIRGIN ISLANDS

| | | |
|---|---|---|
| Black Beard | Santa Cruz $ | .4 |
| Blue Beard | Virgin Islands | .4 |
| Borun's Gold Label | Virgin Islands | .4 |
| Clipper | Virgin Islands | .4 |
| Cruzan | St. Croix | .4 |
| El Dorado | St. Thomas | .4 |
| Government House Rum | Virgin Islands | .4 |
| La Natividad | Virgin Islands | .4 |
| Old St. Croix | Virgin Islands | .4 |
| Old St. Croix Heavy Bodied | Virgin Islands | .4 |
| Pirate's Gold | Virgin Islands | .4 |
| St. Thomas | Virgin Islands | .4 |

### PORTO RICO

| | | |
|---|---|---|
| Beachcomber's | Porto Rico | .4 |
| Brugal Gold Label | Porto Rico | .4 |
| Brugal White Gold | Porto Rico | .4 |
| Daiquiri | Porto Rico | .4 |
| Don Q | Porto Rico | .4 |
| Pellejas Gold | Porto Rico | .4 |
| Pellejas Silver | Porto Rico | .4 |
| Ramirez Royal Superior | Porto Rico | .4 |
| Ron Capito | Porto Rico | .4 |
| Ron Moreno | Porto Rico | .4 |
| Ron Rey | Porto Rico | .4 |

### BARBADOS

| | | |
|---|---|---|
| Barbados Choicest Liqueur | Barbados | .7 |
| Barbados Finest Liqueur | Barbados | .4 |
| Cockade | Barbados | .4 |
| Lightbourn's | Barbados | .6 |
| Punch & Judy | Barbados | .6 |

### FRENCH WEST INDIES

| | | |
|---|---|---|
| Rhum Ara | French West Indies | .4 |
| Rhum Ito | French West Indies | .4 |
| Rhum Negrita | East & West Indies | .4 |

### HAITI

| | | |
|---|---|---|
| Rhum Sarthe | Haiti | .4 |

### TRINIDAD

| | | |
|---|---|---|
| Seigert's Bouquet Rum | Port of Spain | .45 |

### U.S.A.

| | | |
|---|---|---|
| Beachcomber's | New Orleans | .40 |
| Pontalba | Louisiana | .40 |
| Felton's Crystal Springs | New England | .50 |
| Pilgrim Rum | New England | .40 |
| Treasure Cove (20 years old) | New England | .75 |

### PHILIPPINES

| | | |
|---|---|---|
| Rhum Ayala | Philippines | .40 |
| Rhum Tanduay | Philippines | .40 |

### HAWAII

| | | |
|---|---|---|
| Waikiki Brand Rum | Hawaii | .40 |

### PERU

| | | |
|---|---|---|
| Cartavio | Peru | .45 |

List on rums in the Rum Cellar

Havana, Cuba was another of his favorite haunts. Don often visited Havana in order to purchase Cuban rhums and Cuban cigars. Being a great lover and a true aficionado of cigars, he would visit cigar manufacturers in order to make personal selections from the various tobacco leaves. During the first visits to these cigar-making establishments, he was greatly impressed at the quiet, which always hung over the room where the cigar rollers sat at their desks. These desks faced towards the front of the room where a reader stood at a lectern and read from the classics. This quiet and calm, in Don the Beachcomber's opinion, produced some very fine cigars.

*On one of my visits I noticed that the reader had disappeared and light classical music had been introduced. The cigars produced during the reader's absence were still of good quality, but not as expertly rolled as before. Over subsequent visits the music escalated to rock and roll, and the cigars produced no longer resembled the original product. I also noticed a distinct reduction of the quality of the product. However, the Cuban cigar still remained my favorite, and the quality of the tobacco was un-paralleled.*

*One of the damndest things that ever happened to me was when the trade embargo was placed on Cuba after the Castro revolution. This completely interrupted my cigar supply as I could no longer make purchases in Havana. Racking my brain I began to develop an intriguing idea. While traveling to Hong Kong and Tahiti I arranged for shipments of the finest Havanas. In both of these locations the Cuban cigars were legally imported, and a couple of tobacconist friends of mine would remove the Cuban bands and replace them with those of a Filipino product, El Conde De Guelle. The cigars were then re-packaged, and re-boxed as Filipino cigars and either shipped to me in Honolulu, or brought in from Hong Kong by two trusted friends, Bob Allen and Pete Wimberly. I never had one bit of trouble with Customs officials, and Bob and Pete's recompense was dinner in my Treehouse in the center of Waikiki at the International Market Place.*

# Fresh Mint

In early 1939, Don the Beachcomber worked many eighteen-hour days, and he decided on a much needed vacation in Honolulu. When he arrived, he rented a cabana on the beach at the base of Diamond Head for seventy-five dollars a month. It had two bedrooms, a living room and bar, a lanai, kitchen and a bath.

Each time a ship arrived from the west coast of the United States, friends from Hollywood would drop by and expect to be entertained in the same manner they were accustomed to at his Hollywood Don the Beachcomber restaurant and his Plantation in Encino. By the time summer came around Don found himself in need of a staff to help with the cooking. A newspaper ad led to the hiring of two young Japanese girls from a cooking school class who were eager to learn the tricks of the trade. Their pay was eight dollars a week. At four dollars a week, he hired one of the girl's father as caretaker and driver.

*Although I had done a bit of bootlegging in Los Angeles during prohibition after my odyssey around the world, smuggling was a bit new to me. On the occasion of my arrival in Honolulu I found it impossible to locate certain fresh herbs, and I must emphasize the need for the word 'fresh' because dried herbs just wouldn't work with my style of cooking, or for use as condiments in my tropical rhum drinks.*

In his search throughout the Honolulu area, he was able to scrounge up several of the various vegetables necessary for the exotic lunch and dinner dishes his guests expected, but mint for the drinks was another story entirely.

When he was ready to return from Hollywood one day after a supply safari, Don discovered to his consternation that certain items were banned from importation into the Territory of Hawai`i when an agricultural inspector confiscated his prized possessions. He paced through the Pan American Clipper departure lounge and removed his hat in order to scratch his head.

*Suddenly it dawned on me. Why not?, I asked myself.*

Don's plane was due to leave within a couple of hours, and he desperately needed—*"those damn things, especially the mint."* With this in mind, he raced out of the lounge and through the airport, hailed a cab, and went to the nearest store where he purchased seeds and a few small sprigs of mint. He ran to the waiting cab, jumped into the back seat and stuffed the sprigs and seeds into his hatband. When he arrived at the Pan American Clipper lounge, he proceeded immediately and unnoticed onto the plane just in time for take-off.

In Honolulu, there was no problem whatsoever. After he cleared customs, Don went immediately to a telephone, called his Japanese gardener, and asked him to please stop by as soon as he could. When the gardener arrived at Don's Villa, Don presented the man with his loot and told him that he would purchase all he could grow. The gardener had never seen fresh mint before, and he said he didn't know how it would fair in the rich Hawaiian soil. But, he took the booty home with him right away. Some time later Don's investment began to pay off as fresh mint began to arrive at his doorstep. Soon after that, he realized customs wasn't the real problem. Now he received much more mint than he could possibly use.

*And, I couldn't store it, either, because the freshness would soon dissipate and it would be useless to me.*

Don the Beachcomber was not a man to go back on his word, so he suggested to his gardener that he should sell some of it to other people around town.

*Now here was an item I should have kept better control of because, if I had, I would have made a pretty penny off of that one hatband of contraband.*

Don's gardener would always thank him as this adventure turned out to be an economic boon.

# A New Career

While in Honolulu Don opened a new office of the Trade Winds Trading Company. During this same trip a chap by the name of George Pease came into Don's life. Pease said he was an officer with Naval Intelligence, and he told Don he needed a cover.

*I never knew if George Pease was his real name. Anyway, the Trade Winds Trading Company was perfect. Running the store while I was back in Hollywood, Pease had a wonderful opportunity to get the lay of the land while assisting in the greeting of arriving tourist to the island with a station wagon and fresh flower leis.*

The grand opening of Don's Chicago Don the Beachcomber restaurant caused him to travel back and forth between Hollywood, Honolulu and Chicago. The new restaurant had been anticipated by citizens of the Windy City, and lines of customers often formed outside in the drifting snowstorm to wait for a place to stand inside in order to wait for a table or a seat at the bar. This was where Don the Beachcomber first developed his connections with members of the Chicago mob, men who would later contribute to his personal wealth.

In early 1941 Don was about to open another restaurant, this time on Kuhio Avenue in Honolulu. A lot of time and effort had been expended on the details of a fifty-five year lease, and in the end with a $5,000 deposit the deal was closed.

Don hired an architect by the name of Roy Kelley, and plans began to be developed for a twenty-two room Beachcomber hotel with a bar and restaurant on the ground floor. Then, in November, an urgent call came from George Pease. He told Don to *get out from under that lease on Kuhio.* Dumbfounded, but trusting Pease, Don blindly followed the advice. He lost his $5,000 deposit and flew back to Hollywood.

*Major Jimmy Doolittle was a friend of mine, and in February 1942 I received a letter from Washington informing me that I was being commissioned as a Captain in the U.S. Army Air Corps. Thanks to Jimmy, I was to open messes and officer's clubs at Army Air Corps Training Commands in California, Texas, Arizona and New Mexico.*

After spending six months in Santa Ana, another letter came from Doolittle. He expressed his need for Don's expertise in the Mediterranean Theater of Operations. Six more months went by during his stay at a CCC Camp at Carlsbad before he was told by his commander, General Ralph Cousins, that he was to be shipped out for Newport News. On arrival at Newport News, he found a convoy formed up and ready for the voyage to Casablanca.

Captain Don Beach-Comber

*My sea legs never failed, but four German U-boats did their best to sink the entire convoy. When the first torpedo hit our Liberty Ship, I was thrown against a steel bulkhead, cracking three ribs and dislocating my right shoulder. Our ship limped into Casablanca where we were taken to a French evacuation center just outside the city for body repair and recuperation.*

*My rooming companion on board, a Major, who had a lucrative medical practice in Beverly Hills, was also injured, and he was taken with me to this old broken down French Hospital. The huge bed bugs, mosquitoes and bad food increased our desire to recuperate as quickly as possible and join our commands in Lamarsa, near Algiers.*

*During the recuperation period, we were allowed to see the sights of Casablanca. The Major and I headed for the bistros for good wine and good food, but we could find only mediocre wine and poor food. At any of the cafes we visited, we noticed the food was very bland, and we were told by the waiters that the chefs had no pepper or other spices.*

*While walking around the port we discovered a 'Gold Mine,' two United States Navy supply ships.*

*Tall wire fences surrounded the docks where the supply ships were, and the gates, of course, were tightly guarded. Not discouraged, we ran into an Ensign just outside the gate and offered to buy him a drink and show him the sights. During some close questioning and a few drinks, the Ensign volunteered the information we wanted. The ships were filled with all sorts of good things. And, they would be in port unloading for a week. Also, much to our delight, the Ensign turned out to be an assistant to the Officer in Charge of supply and loading.*

*The Major and I immediately planned to liberate some choice items from one of those ships.*

*During our stay in the French hospital, we had become friends with the Sergeant who was in charge of Emergency Room supplies, and who drove the ambulance. With a little talk and a bottle of good cognac, the Sergeant agreed to join our little conspiracy. The Ensign onboard was scheduled to be in total charge of the Supply Room on Sunday. Two days before the raid was to take place he had agreed to show us where the items we wanted were located. Our main problem was getting past the guarded main gate.*

*On Sunday after acquiring the proper medical insignias and uniforms, we piled into the ambulance. Complete with starched sheets and sirens wailing, we arrived at the main gate at about six-thirty in the morning. I jumped out of the ambulance and explained to the guard at the gate that the Captain of one of the ships had to be taken to the hospital. The gate flew open and the three of us continued to the ship unmolested. Arriving at the gangplank, the Sergeant and I grabbed the stretcher and we rushed up and onto the supply ship.*

*At six-thirty on Sunday morning very few crew hands were around or visible. We quickly located the locker storage rooms and found our*

*Ensign friend who was surprised we had gotten as far as we had. I had previously given him a prepared list of our marketing needs at the last bistro we visited. He showed us through the huge doors to the main storage room. Here we selected three smoked hams, one gallon of mayonnaise, thirty-six large apples, three boxes of Hershey bars, two tins of black pepper, one-half pound of thyme and one-half pound of oregano as well as five pounds of spaghetti. On the stretcher, one ham made the sick Captain's head and the other two the stomach area. To construct the rest of the Captain's body I asked the Ensign to loan us two pillows. After everything was draped and tucked in with one of the starched sheets we ran back down the gang plank, loaded the ambulance, and with sirens wailing we raced through the open main gate. We were back in the hospital room before most of the staff was awake. We stuffed our loot under our cots and the Sergeant returned the stretcher. We were having breakfast in the mess hall by seven-forty five.*

*In trading, we made the rounds of various restaurants and cafes with our menus. A measure of black pepper or spice rolled up in one cigarette paper was worth one bottle of good cognac. One apple equaled a four-course lunch or dinner. Two tablespoons of mayonnaise were worth one bottle of good French wine.*

*Let's just say that the Sergeant, the Major and I ate well for the next ten days. And, when we left Algiers we had our ham steak for future eating and trading. My beachcombing days really started in Casablanca and have never ended.*

# Invasion Italy

When he arrived at 12th Air Forces Headquarters at Lamarsa near Algiers, Don joined up with Lieutenant General Jimmy Doolittle.

*The scolding from Doolittle for my tardiness was brief, after which I received the good news. I was to join the push into Italy. As soon as Bari was clear, my duties were to search out and locate suitable areas on the Adriatic coast for the new headquarters of the combined 12th and 15th Air Forces. Also, I was to requisition the best hotels, buildings and villas for rest areas.*

One week later, Doolittle issued Captain Don Beach-Comber a C-47, a crew, seven hundred dollars in gold and a Colt 45. The orders were clear. Set up rest camps for combat weary airman of the 12th and 15th Air Forces in Capri, Nice, Cannes, Venice, the Lido and Sorrento.

*"The gold,"* Doolittle said, *"is just in case you get captured. It may serve to extricate you."*

On the flight over Bari, Captain Beach-Comber watched the Germans move north, out of the city. The C-47 circled until a landing area in an open field was spotted several miles from the city. This was where he would disembark.

Once on the ground, he took off alone and on foot for the heart of the city.

*As I reached the line of tall trees off to the side of our landing area, I heard the outburst of rifle fire. In an instant, I turned to look back expecting to see the C-47 begin to lift-off. To my horror, I watched the plane struggle with smoke coming from one of the engines. It was easy to see the aircraft would not clear the trees in front of it. The crew was in* deep trouble. In only a matter of moments my transportation would crash and burn, and the surviving American crewmembers would be at the mercy of the Fascisti soldiers.

This wasn't Captain Beach-Comber's only problem. Because he had unwittingly stopped and stood in an open field instead of keeping his head down and to make his way into the thick underbrush, some of the Fascisti had taken note of his position and began to move in his direction.

*Alone in the fold of enemy territory and facing my worst fears, I decided I could be of no help to my fellow GIs who would have to fend for themselves. Seeing the whites of their eyes, I darted into the trees and bushes the moment Fascisti rifle fire began to slam into the branches and leaves all around me. At this point, I knew it would be nothing more than a matter of luck to make it another fifty feet before one of bullets, the one with my name on it, found its way home. Before I had sense enough to do what the one training film I saw had taught me to do, I felt a burning sensation in my right shoulder. This helped to revive my meager Carlsbad combat training and I hit the deck. Scrambling on hands and knees, I managed to discover a weed and vine covered hole in the side of a small ditch. Here I hid, not knowing the Fascisti were many times within ten to fifteen feet of my new abode. It was not long before a very loud explosion resounded in the background. It would be the C-47. It was my deepest hope the crew had escaped.*

*With the explosion, I was no longer the center of attention, but I determined I would spend the rest of the day right there in my den. My concern was for my physical condition. As painful as it was, and never having any medical training, I jammed my handkerchief and cloth cap into the wounded area of my shoulder. Luckily, the bullet had passed completely through the fleshy part. It was a clean wound, and I hoped that my attempt at first aid would suffice. The rest of the morning passed without incident. I was not discovered, and once my courage returned, I gingerly exited my hiding place and began to move painstakingly towards Bari. When nightfall approached, I could feel the weight of the day's excitement had been a real burden. I was extremely tired, and in need of nourishment. For another hour I threaded my way in the direction of where I thought Bari was, every now and then ducking behind the nearest rocky outcrop when I heard footsteps. It was only later when I discovered those footsteps were German soldiers looking to give themselves up to any American they came across. I could have become another Sgt. York and did not know it.*

The next few days and nights were filled with tension and surprise. To stay concealed, he found cover wherever he could. Cold at night and hungry, Captain Beach-Comber did not dare speak to anyone for fear they were the enemy.

*I cussed Doolittle for his ineptitude, and I became determined if I ever got back to friendly territory, I would do so to his face if I ever saw him again.*

As things so often seemed to happen throughout the years, the gods looked down with good fortune on Don the Beachcomber.

*One morning I sat beside a small brook to wash out my wounded shoulder with the fresh water when one of god's lovely creatures stepped from the bushes. She stopped only a few feet from my position, and she wasn't the least embarrassed as she removed all of her clothes, stepped into the water and began to bathe. I could only surmise that she had not noticed me. She was a vision of loveliness, the raven-haired beauty with a most remarkable figure. I could do nothing more than watch while she swam and played before she finally turned in my direction and stood waist deep in the brook and smiled at me.*

Captain Beach-Comber's shoulder recovered much more quickly over the next few days because of the attention given him by this Italian farmer's daughter. He ate well from a hidden cache of fine wine and cheeses and other foodstuffs supplied by his new love.

*While I was a few days late reaching Bari, I felt I had gained an insight into the local culture, and in stature because of my experience.*

*My life was full of thrills and excitement along with the wonderment of my little Italian goddess whom I swore I would return to as soon as the war was over. I was looking forward to my next purple heart.*

# Isle of Capri

A month later in Bari, Captain Beach-Comber received new orders with identical instructions that were to take him across Italy to Sorrento and the Isle of Capri while the British 8th Army pushed the Germans northward.

With General Mark Clark's thrust inland from the Mediterranean towards Naples, Captain Beach-Comber departed Bari and crossed German lines towards Sorrento. When he arrived in Sorrento, he found the city open, and quickly began to requisition the beautiful hotels and villas on the beaches in the name of the 12th and 15th Air Forces.

Next on his list was the lovely Isle of Capri. The Germans had retreated, and for all practicality, they destroyed the harbor of Naples. There were no boats available.

*Looking around, I spotted a man fishing at a distance off the coastline. I secured my ride across the thirteen miles of water to Capri once I coaxed the fellow closer to shore and supplied him with a twenty-dollar gold piece and gasoline.*

In Capri, Captain Beach-Comber met with the assistant Mayor and immediately promoted him to Mayor, to replace the previous Mayor who departed with the Germans in a hospital column headed toward Anacapri.

Major Don Beach-Comber at Villa Vismara overlooking Capri

The new Mayor, Mr. Blanco, guided Captain Beach-Comber to the magnificent Villa Vismara. The villa was a fourteen-room estate with seven baths.

*It would be used by General Doolittle and General Spaatz, as well as my own living quarters and headquarters.*

In the bedroom was a twelve foot by twenty-foot bed with lamps on each of the four corner posts. It was said to have belonged to Mussolini. In another room was a magnificent nine-foot classical European Beckstein grand piano. Here, along with Major Lawrence Combs and Sgt. Joseph Tirello, Captain Beach-Comber discovered several false walls containing a cache of fine liqueurs and wines.

*After months of rotgut whisky we had experienced, everyone awoke the next morning with vigorous hangovers.*

Captain Beach-Comber spent a year on the Isle of Capri and played host to a large number of important people, both civilian and military alike.

*Young American officers and enlisted men flew air force bombers over the environment of the battlefields and cities where the enemy threw up the red-hot flak in an effort to knock them out of the sky. They would return to their base with what was called 'accumulate anxiety' while being somewhat 'flak-happy' at the same time. For these men there wasn't anything more depressing than to return to a drab U.S. Army Airdrome in the Italian winter, especially after so many dangerous missions.*

It was in this terrible environment, an environment filled with bombs and bullets, with scenes of smoke and fire billowing up from below, and with the stench of death all around that Captain Beach-Comber took tremendous pains to give the underpaid, frightened, combat weary war veterans as much pleasure as possible under the circumstances.

The first thing he insisted on was fresh, clean white sheets on beds, not cots. To the battle weary American combat pilots the clean white sheets were the most appreciated item of their stay in his rest camps. The men also sat at dining tables covered with white tablecloths and fine silver place settings.

*I never told anyone where I requisitioned the silverware, tablecloths or bed linens. It was not until long after the war had ended that either Sgt. Tirello or I explained our raid on Torino.*

Major Beach-Comber and Sgt. Joe Tirello (In Jeep) in Torino

This is what happened.

*Confusion reigned supreme at the time throughout all of Italy. After our little group had taken the airfield at Rivioli, we found there was no communications with friendly forces. We tried day and night, and finally, with the assistance of a British officer who had been parachuted in, contact was made with the American OSS. As far as Torino was concerned, the British divisions would not approach the city for fear a situation would be created in which they did not wish to become embroiled. The British realized they would be called on to feed the Italian people in the area with food they did not have. The Americans had not arrived either.*

*Because of the situation, I decided to beat everyone else to the punch. With two jeeps, our little group became the first allies to invade the city of Torino. Upon entering the city, we found the partisans rounding up and even shooting some of the more un-cooperative Fascisti soldiers.*

Fascists soldiers being rounded up in Torino

*Warmly welcomed by girls and cheering crowds with flowers and wine, our invading force of liberating American GIs, Lawrence Combs, Joseph Tirello and I partied for two days and nights before I decided that we had better get on with our mission before the Army came in and screwed up everything. It was at Torino where I met Count Theo Rossi of Martini & Rossi distillery. A deal was struck, and nine C-47's from the troop carrier command were brought in. With trucks scrounged from the local community, we loaded the best wines, brandies, champagne, vermouths and Spumante, all of which Count Rossi had somehow kept hidden from the Germans. There was also bed linen, tablecloths, light bulbs, fine silverware and anything else I could get my hands before we headed for the airfield. Once fully loaded, the pilots' main concern was not German fighters, but whether or not they were going to be able to get off the ground. The C-47's were a 'gift from the gods' for they provided a means of bypassing all of the British and American checkpoints in my quest for the best for the combat weary GIs.*

Captain Beach-Comber also incorporated the aide of a small fishing fleet, which would go far out onto the Mediterranean to catch fresh fish. When he heard of a secret cache of good Scotch whisky in Africa, he commandeered two C-47's in order to search it out. After he liberated the scotch, he brought two full planeloads back from

Leopoldville and Nairobi, *and my guests never again had to drink the rotgut brandy so prevalent in Italy at the time.*

One main feature of his rest camp in Lido was a jukebox with a collection of twelve records. He also sought out and hired unemployed Italian chefs whose last places of employment had been Italian luxury liners and hotels now out of operation due to the war.

*It was fun, and I even had the opportunity to chase down spices in Cairo and avocados on Africa's western coast.*

His friends in Hollywood and Chicago sent him ping-pong balls, records, and anything else he needed that they could get through to him. Captain Beach-Comber's collection of dozens of autographed photographs, sent to him by his friends—Hollywood's great film stars of the era—was always on display for combat weary GIs to look at and enjoy.

# Winston Churchill

In early September 1944 Captain Beach-Comber, who now spelled his first name *Donn,* received word from Doolittle about a very secret, hush-hush meeting being planned for later in the month, and would he prepare for any number of arriving VIPs.

Towards the end of September, two British gunboats landed just below the Villa Vismara. The arrival was planned at the bottom of the hill below the villa so the locals would not see the operation. A commotion ensued below while Donn watched from his second story window of the villa high up on the hill. A small group of British Commandos disembarked and quickly made their way up the steep path to make sure the villa and the grounds were secure. A few days later, early in the morning, Captain Beach-Comber watched another gunboat land. When he looked down through a pair of binoculars, he could see Winston Churchill and Lord Mountbatten struggle up the same steep path the Commandos had previously traversed so easily.

*Churchill looked exhausted. I called for my majordomo, selected a bottle of my finest brandy and two glasses, and sent the majordomo down to meet the Prime Minister and Lord Mountbatten. I watched while Churchill took down a couple of good belts before he raised his eyes heavenward.*

*Finally, when he arrived at the villa, Churchill said to me, "You are an angel of mercy. You saved my life."*

Lord Mountbatten didn't say a word to anyone, and simply pushed past the small group and went straight to bed.

The dignitaries stayed four days while engaged in many conferences with various VIPs coming and going. On the last night after dinner and drinks, everyone retired except Churchill.

*I was standing near the large fireplace when Churchill walked over.*

*"Let's you and I have some of your good rhum," Churchill said. "And one of your fabulous cigars."*

*The two of us sat and talked with no one else around. We talked about many things, wine, girls and interesting places Churchill had been, while never once mentioning the war. Over two hours later, having finished off half a bottle of rhum and two excellent Cuban cigars each, I walked Churchill to his room.*

The next morning before Churchill's departure, Donn overheard the Prime Minister say to one of his aides, *I'm sure we have drunk the Captain's cellar dry. Ask him what he needs to replenish his supply.*

After Donn informed the British Prime Minister of his most pressing needs, Churchill promptly shook his hand and said, *You have been a great host. I will send you some potables when I get back to London.*

True to his word, two months later one of those very same gunboats landed below the villa, and Donn watched three British sailors loaded down with wooden cases trudged up the same steep path where Churchill had imbibed in brandy upon his arrival. There was a little note stuck to one of the cases of Queen Anne Scotch. It read, *Many, many thanks. I remembered. Signed Churchill.*

# Lt. C. Moonlight

Major Charles "Chuck" Carey, whom Donn served with in Italy, became one of his closest friends and remained so throughout life. Long after the war, Major Carey retired as executive director of Sheraton Hotel Corporation Services at age sixty-five. He went on to become ordained as a Catholic Priest at the Basilica of St Paul in Rome, and later became a Monsignor in the Catholic Church.

In a letter to his mother written 8 May 1945, Major Carey described scenes and events while his group moved northward towards the front on orders they had received April 28, 1945.

*Major Carey and I, along with Major Lawrence S. Combs and Sgt. Joe Tirello, drove through Pisa and the Italian Riviera along the one lone highway of any consequence. This led to the resort of Rapallo then on to Genoa and Alessandra. Next came the town of Asti where we were the first American troops to arrive. Our advanced party consisted of two jeeps, a trailer and a few rations.*

In his letter, Major Carey wrote:

*Food was our problem. While we brought rations along, they needed embellishment. Donn Beach-Comber is a thoroughly entertaining, unpredictable character, who combines in his restless energetic personality the best attributes of a Maitre d'hotel, and a big time operator who won't take 'no' for an answer. He usually wins out even though his methods may be slightly unethical. We hold our breaths, but everything turns out all right in the end.*

*Donn invariably marches into a kitchen and within minutes has taken over the chef and waiters, if any, and an attractive barmaid whenever possible. The results for the rest of us are most satisfying.*

During this time, Don the Beachcomber developed his abilities as a full-fledged wheeler-dealer, and often became involved in escapades filled with intrigue. He would cajole and use outright bribery to purchase, scrounge for, requisition and trade in *'unique commodities'* for merchandise not openly available to the ordinary Quartermaster.

*Any form of skullduggery and trickery to achieve what I had set out to do on behalf of the soon to arrive GIs and VIPs was never beneath me.*

There were many instances where Donn dealt with black marketeers in order to help local merchants who lent him a hand. Things were 'requisitioned,' and 'requisitioned' most often meant another deal had been struck with the local civilian population, military personnel or Mafia members, some of whom, like the fellow called 'Ramundi,' a man known only by his first name, had been deported from the United States before the war. C-47's were always at Donn's disposal thanks to his friend, Major Lawrence "Larry" Combs.

*Combs issued standing orders to fly me anywhere except to the United States to get whatever I wanted or needed.*

This often meant several days of rest and recreation for Major Combs, Sgt. Tirello and Captain Beach-Comber at the most famous vacation resorts around the Mediterranean. In Cairo, Donn and his trusted sidekick and interpreter, Sgt. Joe Tirello, loaded six United States Army six-by trucks to overflow capacity with Canadian Club and Seagram VO for the flight back to the Isle of Capri. On another excursion, they flew off to the Belgium Congo and achieved the same satisfactory results.

*I made deals with Guiseppi Alberti owner/operator of a local distillery in Benevento famous for Strega Liqueur. Alberti would make up twenty gallons of Strega, and one hundred gallons of gin and cognac at a time in trade for steel girders to rebuild his bombed-out factory. The Army medical staff in Naples cleared this brew as fit to drink for certain undisclosed concessions. The British Navy transported bottles of water and other merchandise to the Isle of Capri for certain visitation rights to the Capri Rest Center.*

Franciscan Monks were used as decoys in order to take two hundred cases of black market Grande Capitan, a Spanish brandy, through British and Canadian checkpoints. A consignment of Provolone Cheese and a farmer's daughter was obtained at a farm just outside Potenza, Italy.

When word got out about cash payments for merchandise, a full Colonel from the Inspector General's Office arrived in Naples to inspect Captain Beach-Comber's books.

*A couple of bottles of dry vermouth on General Barton's desk were enough to send the Colonel on his way with a satisfactory report. Requisitions for cooking equipment and food were issued to local merchants, which were redeemable when the war was over. Lt. C. Moonlight, a man soon promoted to Captain, signed the requisitions.*

*Everyone knew I had a knack for accomplishment, and of getting around army rules and regulations in a manner no one else could. When our fleet of three jeeps was about to give out, I made another deal requiring a night excursion into an area where newly arrived, but unassembled jeeps were being put together. After we exchanged the hoods where all of the serial numbers were located, we drove the old jeeps into the sea, and drove the new jeeps back to Naples. Anything left unprotected was not safe from my itchy fingers.*

# 2,000 Diamonds

In the last days of Germany's hold on Italy, Captain Beach-Comber became involved in one of the more dangerous episodes of his military career.

*Although the war had changed the lives of many people, Contessa Anna had retained her composure and elegant bearing. When I first met the Contessa it was only minutes after someone had stolen my jeep. Many women were anxious to leave the city for Rome, which was now under allied control. One afternoon as I was leaving the Villa Vismara, the Contessa grabbed hold of my arm.*

Coolly, and in perfect English, the Contessa, a confirmed German sympathizer, began to tell Donn of her sister's plight, and of her own strong desire to get the younger girl to Rome. She said her sister wanted to locate a captured German General who had beaten and raped her so she could press charges against him with the Americans. Contessa Anna pleaded not for herself, and said she had no desire to leave to city she loved so much.

*I took her by the arm and assisted her to a small room off the hotel's kitchen. Here she produced a small fortune in fine jewelry as payment for her sister's trip. I estimated the value of the treasure at over twenty thousand American dollars.*

Although he agreed to the deal, Captain Beach-Comber suspected her story did not ring true. He called on Major Combs and met privately with the Contessa and her sister later in the evening. Under interrogation, they discovered the sister's true relationship with the General. They had been lovers. The younger girl said she wanted to be as close to him as possible in order to plead for his release.

Shortly after sunrise the next day, Captain Beach-Comber noticed the two women making a determined effort not to be noticed while they moved through the deserted streets.

*They both seemed to be more than a little ruffled to say the least.*

Donn made his way to the street to block their path, surprised them and guided them into the hotel once again. The two women sat on a cot in the corner of the Headquarters room where the interrogation of the pervious night had taken place. Using chocolate as bait, Captain Beach-Comber uncovered some very special information. The Germans were moving the art treasures of Italy via train through the Brenner Pass. The Contessa's sister, like herself, had not only been a General's lover, but a Nazi sympathizer and collaborator as well. Both women feared for their lives, and the only way to escape punishment at the hands of the town's people would be to leave.

*Upon hearing about the art treasures, I arrested the sister, and immediately sent word to the 12th and 15th Air Forces to bomb the trains, striking only the engines.*

That afternoon in a jeep borrowed from Major Combs, with the Contessa's broken sister seated at his side, Captain Beach-Comber was ready for the trip south. There he would release her into the hands of the allies.

*Not long after we left the city we found ourselves surrounded by a group of armed Fascisti. They closed in, and one of them pulled me from the jeep and waved a revolver under my nose. Then, he recognized the Contessa's sister for who she was, and three of other men grabbed her and began a body search. It was not long before they had discovered a cache of more than two thousand diamonds hidden in her clothes.*

*I immediately mentally kicked myself for missing this treasure.*

*The soldiers looked to one another, and then one of them shot her in the head. He then turned menacingly in my direction but instead of pulling the trigger, he spoke in perfect English. He had noticed my total surprise at the discovery of the diamonds and asked where my unit was and where I was heading. At this point, I quickly realized I was dealing with another 'Ramundi' and a band of enterprising fellows. I mentioned Ramundi's name, plus the names of a few others I had had dealings with in Chicago at my Beachcomber Restaurant. It was not but a minute later before I was pulling out a few bottles of my prime scotch from the back of the jeep and a deal was struck. These fellows gave me several of the diamonds for my trouble and released me. I immediately started up the jeep, turned around and drove straight back to Naples. I have always been happy I never ever saw or heard of those chaps again.*

# Bouillabaisse

In late 1944, orders came for Sgt. Joe Tirello and Major Beach-Comber to return to southern France to search of a new Headquarters and Rest and Recreation area.

On the French Riviera Don the Beachcomber drove along a palm lined thoroughfare in Cannes where he visited many fine hotels before he finally stopped at the luxurious Carlton Hotel. The American GIs tramped into the lobby and the manager began to shout, *"Mon Dieu, they are here. The tourists have returned."*

When Don received a list of the most desirable hotels and villas from the hotel manager, he made the rounds with Sgt. Tirello before he finally selected the Hotel Martinez as site of the 12th Air Forces new Headquarters.

Major Don Beach-Comber (Right) in front of Hotel Martinez—Cannes Rest Camp—WWII

*The following day Joe and I drove to Cap D'Antibes to look for suitable villas for use as living quarters for Generals Doolittle and Spaatz, and for Major Combs and myself. Once again, I found myself landing in the lap of luxury.*

While Major Beach-Comber and Sgt. Tirello drove along the narrow road, Donn spotted a beautiful villa right smack on a little beach. A pool had been carved out of the rocks in front. He asked Sgt. Tirello to stop, and he climbed down and walked through the opening in a rock-walled garden to knock on a handsomely carved door.

*Almost instantly, it was opened by a haughty majordomo type gentleman of about fifty who appeared much surprised. I introduced myself and told him I wanted to inspect his villa.*

The name on the gate was Aujourdui. The man was quick to explain that the owner, an English woman by the name of Mrs. Williams, had left the Riviera for England just before the Germans arrived. He, Andre Lochier, was charged with the care of her villa. Major Beach-Comber asked Mr. Lochier to take him through the rooms.

*There were seven beautifully decorated rooms, each of a different color and design. The kitchen was the most complete kitchen I had ever seen. While we were standing in the kitchen, the Mr. Lochier stated that he had also cooked for Mrs. Williams. At this point, I became very interested. I asked him what his specialty was and he said that he made splendid soufflés. I was sure I wanted to requisition the villa Aujourdui for myself, for today I would start to enjoy the war.*

Sgt. Tirello and Major Beach-Comber also stopped in Nice and located a little restaurant on the beach, but found it closed with a card on the door featuring the chef/owner's home telephone number. Donn called the man and asked if he would come down to the restaurant and meet with him as he had an important matter to discuss. Thirty minutes later the man appeared. Major Beach-Comber introduced himself and the two of them went in.

*I asked him if he could prepare a bouillabaisse. He revealed that seafood had not been available for months and reminded me of the German mines in the waters just off Nice. He said his name was Jean-Paul, and he revealed that he owned a small boat but had no petrol. He did say if he had five gallons of petrol he and a friend could sneak through the mine fields and find the seafood he needed. I asked Jean-Paul if he could find a salad, an appetizer, and if I gave him the necessary items for French bread and dessert, could he put together a bouillabaisse dinner worthy of his reputation. He was delighted.*

Major Beach-Comber wrote out a menu for four as he wanted two ladies to join them in the sumptuous meal Jean-Paul would prepare. He gave the man his telephone number at headquarters, and suggested that as soon as he was ready, he should call so the two of them and the two ladies could enjoy Major Beach-Comber's martinis.

Four days later Major Beach-Comber received the telephone call. Jean-Paul asked Donn to come to the back door of his establishment, as he did not wish for the lights to be on for others to see and be curious. He described the two ladies as being young, beautiful and eager.

When Major Beach-Comber arrived, he noticed candles and flowers on the small kitchen table, and the man's description of the seated guests was more than accurate.

*The two girls appeared to be shy, and quite young. I made the martinis for my host and myself. The girls took an aperitif. The appetizer was served.*

Major Beach-Comber's host then brought out a beautiful hot, crusty baguette. The girls looked at the host as if to ask for permission to eat. When he nodded, they tore into the bread and devoured the appetizer.

The bouillabaisse arrived in a large copper pot and Jean-Paul placed it at the center of the table. Then, he ladled the portions. The girls seemed starved. Jean-Paul filled the soup bowls a third time, poured an excellent wine and served the desert, a superb chocolate soufflé.

*Dinner over, I offered Jean-Paul one of my good cigars. He brought a bottle of cognac and we sipped on Nescafe coffee I had remembered to bring.*

*During the meal, I noticed the girls glancing at my host seemingly anxious. Previously I had explained to Jean-Paul that after dinner I would take him and the girls back to my villa at Cap de Antibes for a swim, and to listen to some American records I had scrounged. This seemed agreeable.*

*We had eaten everything in sight, so, after our cigars, brandy and liqueurs I was ready to go to the villa and suggested that it was time to start. The girls appeared fearful and spoke with Jean-Paul in rapid French. At this point, Jean-Paul asked if I would step into the dining room as he had something very important he must tell me.*

*In the darkened room, he took my hands, and in a broken voice said, "Major Beach-Comber, I am so very sorry." At his home, Jean-Paul had described to his family the meeting we had had at his restaurant about the pending dinner arrangements and the two lady dinner guests. Still holding my hands, and with tears in his eyes Jean-Paul said, "Major, these girls are my daughters." He went on to explain that the girls had begged to be the dinner guests.*

*I went back into the kitchen and told the girls I had enjoyed meeting them and being with them, and hoped to see them again.*

*I then drove back to the villa and dove into the pool.*

# *Hawai`i*

After his return home at the end of World War II, Don the Beach-comber tried to make a go of it at his old haunts in Hollywood and Encino, and in Chicago, but found many things had changed, and the changes were not to his liking. While his employees were happy to see him return, there were others, including his wife, Cora Irene "Sunny" Sund, who weren't. His life was so drastically changed, and now devoid of the excitement of the adventurous days in Italy and France, the enjoyment his rest camps had given to so many battle weary flyers still in his mind, Don the Beachcomber set out for the one place he loved so much, Hawai`i.

*The only thing I was able to take from my years of work was the rights to the name Don the Beachcomber for Hawai`i, Asia and the South Pacific.*

Don rented a room at the Royal Hawaiian Hotel, and searched out a location for a new restaurant. He didn't have to look far because just across from the Royal Hawaiian Hotel sat an empty expanse of land on the mauka or mountain side of Kalakaua Avenue.

*The vice-president of Matson Navigation was a very delightful man, and a very generous one to me.*

On a one-acre parcel of this prime real estate, Don the Beach-comber signed a lease at two hundred-fifty dollars a month. The Queen's Royal Gardens was a vast empty area with little more than a few coconut trees. This is where Macy's sits today—2007—next door to the International Market Place.

He always looked for ways to turn the romance, adventure and intrinsic allure of the South Pacific into dollars and cents. Donn enlisted the assistance of his friend and architect, Pete Wimberly, whom he had first met years before in his original *Don's Beachcomber* bar on McCadden Place. With his knowledge of Polynesia, and Pete Wimberly's skills as an architect, the two men designed a new South Pacific Village on the order of Donn's Encino Plantation.

In February of 1947, construction of the tropical village, which consisted of three Tahitian style thatched long houses, began. The first longhouse, *Don's High Talking Chief's Hut,* was especially designed and lavishly decorated from Don's personal collection of south sea treasures. This building would be used for private *Feasts of the Islands* parties. Next came *The Beachcomber's Crossroad Bazaar.* Arts and crafts of Hawai`i, Tahiti, Samoa, Philippines, China, Japan and India were featured. Here guests could find some of the most rare and different trade goods, and see Donn's collection of giant man-eating clam shells. The third longhouse was *'The Tahitian Dining Hut'* where Donn prepared exquisite Cantonese cuisine, and where many of his original tropical rhum drinks were served daily.

The original Don the Beachcomber Restaurant in Waikiki

*We landscaped the property with water ponds, ferns, palms and other assorted flowers and plant life to create a masterpiece. This is where my 'Don the Beachcomber' style of tourism really came to life in Waikiki.*

*From the onset of construction, a woman by the name of Madam Zahirhelli, the Governor's paramour, led a fight to halt my project. She insisted the Pandanus leaves covering the exterior of the buildings made them extremely susceptible to fire, and demanded the Fire Marshall inspect my operation in order to shut it down. Late one evening towards the end of construction, I received an anonymous warning call from a friend inside the Honolulu Fire Department. The next morning the fire brigade arrived to look things over. Demonstrating just how safe Pandanus actually was, I took a torch and tried to set one of the buildings on fire. Fortunately, the flames did not take hold and the Pandanus leaves did not burn. I was relieved when the Fire Marshall signed the certificate giving my buildings a clean bill of health. He never knew that I had thoroughly watered everything down before the fire brigade arrived.*

Some of the more recognizable beneficiaries of this episode became the Polynesian Cultural Center, Paradise Cove Luau and Germaine's Luau, along with the Kona Village on the big island of Hawai`i.

Here at his South Pacific Village, Donn put on first-rate luaus that became legendary. They were the first commercial luaus presented in Hawai`i. However, not just anyone could attend. One had to have a personal invitation from Don the Beachcomber.

*Of course, if you knew me, or if you were staying at the Royal Hawaiian Hotel, the invites came automatically with your arrival in Honolulu.*

No one knew how to throw a party any better than Don the Beachcomber. His years of doing business in Hollywood and Chicago, along with his experiences in Italy and France during the war, and most of all the experience of the many luau he held at his Encino Plantation fully prepared him for the success to follow.

Dressed in a traditional wide brimmed Tahitian Pandanus hat, Don the Beachcomber sported a bare chest with a necklace of wild boars tusks and a maile lei around his neck. A lava-lava covered him from the waist down. With bare feet completing the picture, he presented an unexpected but pleasant sight for the eyes of the many visitors to the islands who came to his Sunday *Feast of the Islands Luau.*

Don the Beachcomber in Sunday night luau attire

Right from the onset, Donn seized on opportunities no one else recognized. His music was live and authentic. All of his musicians, singers and dancers were drawn from the local community. Such richly talented entertainers as Alfred Apaka, Rosalie Stevenson, Haunani Kahalewai and Iolani Lauhine to mention a few, performed to the best of their abilities to the delight of the happy, appreciative malihini and locals alike. A cast of over forty, which included the *Beachcomber Serenaders,* joined in the performance along with a fifteen-member orchestra.

Alfred Apaka

Not only was Hawaiian music and hula performed, but Don the Beachcomber was the first to import singers, dancers and musicians from another of his favorite haunts, Tahiti. Anna Gobreght was the first. Anna danced under the name *Manuana,* which means *bird from the cave,* for four years at the *High Talking Chief's Hut* and at the Don the Beachcomber Sunday luau.

Anna 'Manuana' Gobreght

*At the time immigration officials didn't seem to know the difference between a Tahitian singer/dancer/entertainer from a Hawaiian singer/*

*dancer/entertainer. Many local artists and musicians did not want any imports, and most thought local artists would suffice. They fought against this new, radical idea. But, with the help of a letter from the curator of the Bishop Museum, Mr. Kenneth Emory, I got my way and soon people were lined up to see the shows.*

For lunch and dinner Don the Beachcomber followed a successful formulae of his original exotic tropical rhum drinks combined with Chinese food dishes, mostly his own renditions.

Scene from original Don the Beachcomber Sunday night luau in Waikiki

*Like my Plantation luau in Encino, the Sunday luau in Waikiki were as authentic as one could get, and not like the commercial Arkansas picnics you see throughout the islands today.*

*I conducted these lavish luau for ten years on the grounds of the tropi-cal gardens Pete Wimberly and I created. Here invited guests, paying customers, for I asked a donation of twelve dollars, were seated on the ground dressed in as authentic Polynesian attire as they could possibly conger up for themselves. Prayers were offered over a roasting pig before it was pulled from the imu to the delight of the unsuspecting audience. On a typical moonlit tropical evening, spectators were given the impression they were witnessing a pig worshiping ceremony in Tahiti as selected guests were required to kiss an ear before the feast began.*

# The Original Mai Tai

It was at the original Don the Beachcomber Restaurant in Waikiki at the *High Talking Chief's Hut* where a very special Original Beachcomber tropical rhum concoction, first served at Don's Beachcomber bar in Hollywood in 1933, was re-introduced to the public in Hawai`i. This drink was the Mai Tai. The Mai Tai has since became so well known and popular worldwide that boats have been named after it. Restaurants, nightclubs and bars have been named after it, and of all the original exotic tropical rhum drinks Don the Beachcomber ever created, it remains the most popular among the many millions of tourists and visitors to the islands.

*There continues to be controversy over who originally came up with the Mai Tai. It has never bothered me that Vic Bergeron took credit, and I have never held a grudge. The plain fact is, there can be no truer form of flattery than when other people claim credit for your concepts and ideas and use them to their own benefit. This happened many times throughout my life, and there are no grudges held.*

This it how it was with Vic Bergeron, a.k.a. Trader Vic, whom Donn the Beachcomber often thought of as his star pupil and best imitator, and the man who for years claimed to be the originator of the Mai Tai in 1944 while sailing in Tahiti.

*Vic eventually admitted I invented the drink. In a letter to Don Chapman of the Honolulu Advertiser, the well-known Syndicated Columnist Jim Bishop, who knew both Vic Bergeron and I quite well, wrote the following regarding who invented the Mai Tai.*

# Don Chapman. . .

Beach                    Alexander

ROLLING SEVEN-ELEVEN: We have here what could be the final word on who really created the *mai tai*, "**Donn the Beachcomber**" **Beach** or "**Trader Vic**" **Bergeron**. Both men, who have since gone on to that great bar in the sky, publicly claimed to have invented the drink. But **Jim Bishop** recalls sitting with Donn and Vic at Trader Vic's in San Francisco in the early '70s. As Jim tells it, after a number of mai tais, Vic leaned across the table and said: "Blankety-blank Donn, I wish you'd never come up with the blankety-blank thing. It's caused me a lot of arguing with people." Then, says Jim: "Vic looked at me and said, 'Jim, this blankety-blank *did* do it. I didn't'" . . . Where's **Ron Rewald** when we need him to lead the expedition dept.: Young G.I. we know was approached in Waikiki by a fellow trying to sell "a map that shows where **Ferdinand Marcos** buried his millions in the Philippines" for $100. The fellow claimed the map was drawn by family friends, who helped Marcos bury the loot □ □ □

DIS AND DOT: Sure, her int'l modeling career has taken off. But what **Brooke Alexander**, the former Miss World, really wanted to talk about the other day was beating **Jeff Lamp** of the L.A. Lakers in a one-on-one match during **Magic Johnson**'s basketball camp on Maui. Brooke, of course, stands 6-ft.-1 and was a hoops star at Kalaheo before her beauty queen days . . . Gov. **John Waihee** is due to be arrested and jailed on Fri. The jail is at Pearlridge and he'll arrive by limo — then hope that friends and supporters quickly come up with enough money to bail him out — part of the American Cancer Society's Jailathon fundraiser . . . **Dana Costanza**, ladies lounge attendant at Nicholas Nickolas, overheard it the other night: "When it comes to unemployment benefits, you sure can't beat alimony" □ □ □

OVER THERE: **Michael Kliks** is packing his bags for Burkina Faso, the African nation formerly known as Upper Volta, where he'll spend four months on a Fulbright Fellowship. But first Michael is hoping for a big ocean swell by Sat. That's the last day he'll be able to defend his Hawaiian Bodysurfing Championship in the masters div. Michael, whose speciality is Guinea

Don Chapman writes about Jim Bishop's comments about the origin of the Mai Tai
Tuesday—July 11, 1989

Here are the contents of that letter:

*In probably 1970 or '71 Donn and I were with Vic at Vic's in San Francisco.*

*In the friend-foe relationship Donn and Vic had, Vic said in effect that night, "blankety blank, Donn, I wish you'd never come up with the blankety blank thing. It's caused me a lot of arguing with people."*

*Then Vic looked at me and said "Jim, this blankety … blank <u>did</u> do it. I didn't."*

And so, with his own words, Trader Vic settled the question of who invented the Mai Tai. Trader Vic also had the the following printed on one of his menus, … *I salute Don the Beachcomber as the outstanding rum connoisseur of our country.*

But, the argument about who originated the Mai Tai continues to this very day, years after the two men have passed on to the great reward.

Original Secret Recipe for

* * *The Original Mai Tai* * *

For your drinking pleasure

This robust sized rhum drink is to be enjoyed well after the Kona Coffee Grog and throughout the evening. With full-flavored Jamaica rhum, Don the Beachcomber guarantees that this hearty rhum punch will provide comfort, warm your blood and restore your strength.

Into a mixer add:

  1½ oz. Myer's Plantation Rhum
  1 oz. Cuban Rhum
  ¾ oz. fresh lime juice
  1 oz. fresh grapefruit juice
  ¼ oz. Falernum

½ oz. Cointreau
2 dashes Angostura Bitters
1 dash Pernod
Shell of squeezed lime
1 cup of cracked ice (size of a dime)

Shake for one minute on medium speed. Serve in double old fashion glass. Garnish with four sprigs mint. Add a spear of pineapple. Sip slowly through mint sprigs until desired effect results.

# A Waikiki Convention Center

In the late 1940's a longshoreman's strike lasted nine months and reeked havoc on Honolulu's hotel and restaurant community, and even a death blow to a few businesses. At the time all supplies to the Hawaiian islands arrived by Matson ship, even the tourists. Throughout this period, several large department stores in San Francisco had signs in their windows:

*If you have loved ones in the Hawaiian Islands*
*Sent them a care package*

Don the Beachcomber was president of the Restaurant Association in Honolulu at the time.

*As discussions went around about how the strike might be resolved, a fifty thousand dollar payment was seriously considered for a 'cement overcoat' with burial at sea for the man everyone held responsible for the strike, Mr. Jack Hall. Fortunately, for Mr. Hall and all concerned, the strike ended before the plan was carried out. Word on the street was that Mr. Hall had somehow received word of his impending relocation, and he brought the strike to a quick settlement.*

Around this time in talks with Samuel P. King, Governor of the Territory of Hawai`i, Don the Beachcomber was the first to propose construction of a convention center for Waikiki. He suggested it be located on the mauka side of the Ala Wai Canal in conjunction with the Ala Wai Golf Course. Within walking distance of Waikiki, he envisioned three or four pedestrian footbridges to span the canal at various distances. Over the years he continued to stress the importance of the Ala Wai Convention Center concept *'within easy saun-*

*tering distance'* from the vacation hotels of Waikiki. He was always disappointed by the suggestions of others that it be located elsewhere outside Waikiki, and inconvenient to convention goers.

Donn was President of the Waikiki Association. He and a group of civic and business leaders dedicated to the creation of first-class visitor attractions and facilities designed to satisfy the most discriminating, Donn spoke with Governor King about the twelve o'clock bewitching hour for all bars in Hawai`i. With Governor King's okay he managed legislation through the Territorial legislature to extend the hours for bars and hotels to two o'clock in the morning, and for cabarets to four o'clock. Only two ministers offered objections to the legislation that drastically increased profits for so many citizens of Hawai`i, and provided great satisfaction for visitors to the islands.

Then there were the catamarans, the first ones capable of travel to Tahiti from Hawai`i. These were fifty and sixty-foot creations designed for thirty passengers for sunset dinner cruises off the beaches of Waikiki. The boats would be built by Donn's friend, Skip Creager, and himself. However, major unforeseen problems developed with the city government of Honolulu over the embarkation and debarkation of passengers with ladders from the beach in Waikiki, and this idea was abandoned.

Cover of brochure featuring Don the Beachcomber catamarans in Waikiki

*We eventually built smaller catamarans, twenty feet in length, called the 'Waikiki Beachcomber Catamaran' for sale or rental to local residents and visitors to the islands. Tested in the Molokai Channel, these catamarans were capable of reaching speeds of thirty-five knots and sold F.O.B. Honolulu for eight hundred ninety-five dollars. Plans for building your own sold for seventy-five dollars.*

# Bush Beer

*It was once said I was a man who had built a successful career out of being a tropical tramp of the more picturesque persuasion. Tropical tramp, no. Tropical scrounger, yes.*

In December of 1952 while the South Pacific underwent its regular yearly influx of experienced and inexperienced travelers, Don the Beachcomber decided to make a quick jaunt to Tahiti.

*In route, I joined up with a small but delightful group that had descended on this part of the world when the temperatures plummeted towards freezing in their hometowns.*

As a part of a regularly scheduled Circle of the Pacific flight, a Sunderland flying boat made a stop on the magnificent blue-green lagoon of Aitutaki in the Cook Islands. This trip was no different.

*We flew over Aitutaki, and a wide eyed, gasping group of tourist strained for pictures of the beautiful circular atoll of islands with a large enclosed lagoon in the center. Finally, the Sunderland flying boat banked to the left before descending, and the salt-water spray splattered the windows as the plane first bounced and then skimmed the water of the lagoon.*

It was not long before the group waded ashore for an hour or so on the small, uninhabited motu (island) of Akiami while the Sunderland crew refueled the plane. This was a regular fuel stop, but there was no fuel. They were going no further, at least not until tomorrow.

Don the Beachcomber and tourist stranded at Aitutaki in the
Cook Islands

*Akiami was a totally deserted motu. And, there was absolutely no accommodation whatsoever for the plane's passengers. We would be spending the night as castaways, ala 'Swiss Family Robinson.' The nearest township was Aitutaki at a distance much to far for anyone to swim. While we settled down to our predicament, I noticed a fisherman with a small boat off in the distance. I knew he may be curious about the large flying boat sitting in the lagoon, so I got the group together and we began to wave anything we could get our hands on in order to gain his attention. Twenty minutes later, I was on my way to Aitutaki to requisition supplies. When I returned to Akiami I had in my possession enough to create some make-shift accommodations, plus some fish, bread and sweet potatoes. However, there were no vegetables. For drinking, I had been able to get the only thing available, bush beer. Bush beer is a local concoction made of oranges and fermented in the stump of a tree until it has obtained what the locals consider to be the proper potency.*

*Well, we settled in for the duration. An open fire for cooking was lit, and a scrap piece of corrugated metal was used for the stovetop. After exploring the deserted motu of Akiami, and eating a meal to remember and washing it down with the delightful orange bush beer, everyone settled down for a good night's sleep. At about two in the morning I was awakened to the call of nature, and the effects of the Bush beer. There near the scraggly bushes of Akiami on a cloudless night with a full moon, was a line of people with shining rear ends peering out of their lowered pants in the wee hours of the morning.*

*After a rather discomforting night, morning broke with the late arrival of the supply plane with the fuel we needed for our welcome departure from our lovely island stopover.*

Around this time, for 1,600 francs per day, or $26.60 in U.S. dollars, one could enjoy double accommodations and a fabulous stay, all meals were included, on a seven-acre coconut plantation situated along another beautiful blue lagoon. This place was the *Les Tropiques Bungalow—Hotel in Papeete, Tahiti.* It was here with Donn's friend and business associate, Rick Barnes, of Australia, that Donn became the first American to have such an operation in his favorite haunt, Tahiti. Dotted about the enchanted acres were charming and comfortable native style bungalows, which overlooked a blue lagoon with a view of the beautiful island of Moorea in the distance. Vacationers enjoyed native feasts, or *Tama'ara'a* in Tahitian, of exotic foods, they learned various Tahitian dances, and went on picnics and fishing excursions for world record Blue Marlin. Guests could also savor the thrill of a wild pig hunt. A paradise for camera enthusiasts, there were schooner trips to the islands of Moorea and Bora Bora, and Tahitian outrigger canoes were available as rentals for exploration of the beautiful Auae Lagoon.

Of course Don the Beachcomber's famous exotic tropical rhum creations always dressed up the afternoon and evening meals which consisted of French, Chinese and America cuisine, plus Tahitian food specialties. Dancing and romance under star-filled Tahitian nighttime skies, where rhythms of native guitars and exotic drums pulsated. The allure of Donn and Rick's tropical tourist village was unmistakable. For reservations, one only had to wire *Don the Beachcomber on the Beach at Waikiki.*

So popular and well known had the name Don the Beachcomber become that by 1953 Don the Beachcomber made an appearance in the comic strip *'The Saint,'* written by Leslie Chartris and John Spranger. Anyone who read *'The Saint'* knew immediately who this legendary figure was, or at least they thought they did. Take syndicated newspaper columnist, Jim Bishop for instance, who years before had had a $1.25 Mai Tai at *Don's Beachcomber* bar on McCadden Place.

In an article he later wrote about Don the Beachcomber, Jim Bishop said, in part: *I'd look at the menu cover. There was no use looking inside because I couldn't afford both food and the Mai Tai. There was and still is a drawing of Don the Beachcomber on the cover. A mustached man wearing a battered woven hat. Staring out at the farthest horizons. I never dreamed there was a real Don the Beachcomber. Just a drawing I thought. Then at Suva, on the far side of Fiji, the drawing came to life. Don stepped off an old prop passenger plane. The hat was the same. Battered, stained, a heavy shell band. The dark skinned clean cut face was the same. So were the mustache and quick black eyes.*

# The International Market Place

In early 1954, after contacting Paul Trousdale and Clint Murchison to let them in on the *'Deal of the Century,'* Pete Wimberly and Donn Beach stood among the lush tropical luau gardens of his Plantation in Waikiki and drew out the plans for the *'The International Pacific Village and Marketplace,'* on three acres of land in the heart of Waikiki.

*While I used a stick to draw my ideas in the dirt, Pete found a piece of plain brown wrapping paper on which he sketched out the original plans. By June of 1955 the Honolulu Chamber of Commerce approved the plan, and by February 1956 bulldozers were busy clearing the sight across the street from the Royal Hawaiian Hotel in preparation for construction.*

The Pacific Village eventually became known as the *International Market Place.* Here Donn helped to develop the *International Market Place* into an important visitor destination with over forty shops, nine restaurants, tropical gardens, promenades, displays and Polynesian entertainment for the enjoyment of visitors and residents alike. In actuality, this original concept was nothing more than an expanded version of his Encino Plantation.

Entrance to Don the Beachcomber in International Market
Place—Waikiki

Donn knew the upset price ahead of time, thanks to a friend who worked at Queens Hospital. Because of Donn's knowledge, Trousdale and Murchison won out in the bid for the lease of the property against Henry Kaiser and four others.

Construction began and the *International Market Place* was built for a grand total of nine hundred thousand dollars. Thirty years later in 1986, Trousdale was offered sixty million dollars for the lease for same property and would not sell.

Besides being the developer of the concept of the International Market Place, Donn also designed the merchandise formula, and as a result of his efforts, he was given very favorable lease arrangements and considerations. It was not long before a new, larger and more elaborate *Don the Beachcomber Restaurant* was constructed in the International Market Place towards the rear where the Haulau Building is located. At the front entrance to the Market Place along Kalakaua Avenue he built two other buildings, one on each side of the main entrance. The first was the *Colonel's Plantation Beefsteak and Coffee House* and the other a series of small shops.

Ten years to the day from the opening of his original South Pacific Village along Kalakaua Avenue, the old place was torn down and Don the Beachcomber moved into his new headquarters.

To liven things up a bit, he imported five talking mynah birds from India and taught them several refinements of the English language. They strolled around the overhangs of his *Dagger Bar* so visitors to the islands could stop and talk with them.

*I called this group of winged predators 'Rajah and the Hill Minors,' and they could speak the following. 'Hello, you dumb shit. How's the bird today? Give me a beer, give me a beer, give me a beer, stupid.' They could laugh and give wolf whistles which always drew someone's attention. Just like my original Rajah in Hollywood years before, Rajah enjoyed the taste rhum, but he would not drink directly from a cup. In order to entertain my guests, I fed Rajah rhum soaked pieces of apple where upon the bird would wobble around before falling off his perch and wander over on the top of the bar before passing out in a drunken stupor.*

The most famous place of all in the *International Market Place* was Don the Beachcomber's *Treehouse for Two*. He built the treehouse in an out of the way location, high up in the one-hundred-year-old banyan tree towards the front entrance of the property. At a total cost of $4,000.00, a treehouse system made of two separate treehouses connected by stairways, was constructed. It was in this secluded and romantic atmosphere where lovers, and the famous and infamous alike from around the world could enjoy a pleasant dinner in their very own private abode. Here they were seduced by the most pleasant of settings while looking out over the waters of Waikiki Beach at sunset. At thirty-five dollars for dinner, fine French champagne at ten dollars, service was fit for a king and queen.

Donn Beach in his Banyan tree treehouse at the International Market Place—Waikiki

Just a few steps away in the same banyan tree was Don the Beachcomber's private office-cum Treehouse Restaurant where he would entertain international visitors for luncheon. Here he introduced friends and business associates to many of his original concepts and designs while he served them his delicious food and original exotic tropical rhum concoctions until their mouths watered and they chomped at the bit to get started. Don the Beachcomber had an unparalleled way with words and was a great storyteller. Many people looked upon the Treehouse as the most exclusive restaurant in the world.

It was here in the International Market Place at Don's small open-air outdoor amphitheater, at the Don the Beachcomber Restaurant, the Colonel's Plantation Beefsteak and Coffee House, and the Dagger Bar where Don encouraged so many local seasoned entertainers, and new, unknown, budding young dancers and singers.

A typical advertisement read in part: *Walk through the International Marketplace to the world-famous Don the Beachcomber Cabaret-Restaurant, where you will enjoy a brilliant Polynesian revue featuring a galaxy of Island stars in primitive dances from Tahiti, ceremonial fire rites of Samoa, songs, chants and hulas of new and old Hawai`i. Dancing under the stars to the music of the Beachcomber Serenaders.*

At these various haunts, you would find the likes of Rosalie Stevenson and James Cagney serenading the cast and crew of the movie *Mr. Roberts*. Queenie Ventura would dance and teach the finer points of the hula to Bob Hope. This is where Martin Denny, Arthur Lyman and Augie Colon first entertained as a group, and where Alfred Apaka first emceed and entertained.

James Cagney and Rosalie Stevenson singing at Mr. Roberts
luau

Bob Hope being taught the hula by Queenie Ventura

Besides the development of exotic tropical rhum concoctions, Don the Beachcomber continually experimented with exotic herbs and spices imported from all over the world.

Waiter in Indian attire

Colonel's Plantation Beefsteak and Coffee House

Whether in attendance at a Sunday evening luau, or at dinner in the *Don the Beachcomber Restaurant*, the *Colonel's Plantation Beefsteak and Coffee House,* or high up in the Banyan Tree with a view to the beach at Waikiki, all meals were prepared and presented to each individual customer as if they were a king or queen, by highly trained staff dressed in East Indian attire with turbans.

# Henry Kaiser

Henry Kaiser, who lost out on the bid for the lease on the International Market Place property, came to Don's restaurant and cabaret with his wife twice a week on regular basis. Kaiser had purchased the property at the intersection of Ala Moana Boulevard and Kalia Road in Waikiki then known as *Niamalu*. Today it is known as the Hilton Hawaiian Village.

During construction of his Hawaiian Village, Henry Kaiser developed plans for a cabaret to be called the *Tapa Room*.

Henry Kaiser and wife with Queenie Venture and Alfred Apaka—Don the Beachcomber—International Market Place—Waikiki

*Well, Henry Kaiser had been a crafty little devil. Making friends, he would ask me questions and pick my brain for ideas. At the same time, he cemented mental pictures of my Don the Beachcomber Restaurant's interior design in his head.*

Alfred Apaka, Rosalie Stevenson, Iolani Luahine, Martin Denny, Arthur Lyman, Queenie Ventura, Augie Colon and others performed nightly at Don's establishments. Henry Kaiser had an idea. When Alfred Apaka spoke with Don on one occasion, he told Don that Kaiser had offered him seven hundred fifty dollars a week to perform at the Hawaiian Village in the *Tapa Room* which was about to open. During this period, Alfred was making top wages of two hundred fifty dollars a week.

*Well, I could only shake my head. Alfred asked me for advice, and I told him to take the money, and tell the old bastard that I'll come too for eight hundred a week.*

Alfred Apaka joined Henry Kaiser at the Tapa Room, and so did Martin Denny and his group that included Arthur Lyman and Augie Colon. But, all of Don's other entertainers like Rosalie Stevenson told Kaiser to shove it. Not one of the bartenders went, nor did any of the other employees. Don the Beachcomber had always been more than fair with his employees, and now they showed their respect and refused Kaiser's generous offers. As for those who did take advantage of the money Kaiser offered, Don the Beachcomber never held a grudge against any of them, and wished them well.

Kaiser copied every one of Don the Beachcomber's ideas down to the last pandanas leaf and motorized Indian punkah (fan).

*But that punkah brought Henry Kaiser problems, and I felt vilified.*

*Opening night the Tapa Room was filled with dancing, fun and laughter, food and drinks. A full house watched and listened while Alfred Apaka performed to his magnificent best. As the evening progressed, a steel rod operating Kaiser's rendition of my Indian punkah snapped. Swinging wildly from one end it hit a woman visitor in the back and broke her shoulder blade. The woman sued Kaiser for thirty thousand dollars, and the old man quickly paid off.*

In the end, Don wrote Kaiser a letter, which said:

*My Dear Mr. Kaiser;*

*I understand you have broken your punkah. I come from a long line of punkah makers and will repair it for you for $30,000.00.*

*Respectfully, Donn Beach.*

There was, of course, no answer to the letter.

*Over the years, I have become disenchanted,* Donn said later in life. *It broke my heart to see what greed has done to change the face of the International Market Place. The true Polynesian atmosphere is completely destroyed. The delightful ambiance I had so successfully created has turned into a conglomeration of displays of geeaws with the incessant sounds of hawkers doing little more than attempting to peddle their merchandise.*

# Pearls and Pineapple

One of Don the Beachcomber's best design concepts was the famous pearl carts. These were the first merchandise kiosks built and used in Hawai`i. He placed the original just outside the entrance of the Colonel's Plantation Beefsteak and Coffee House at the International Market Place where he was also the first in Hawai`i to offer aged, chilled beef along with European style coffee. The idea for the Pearl Carts came from one of Don's original rhum concoctions called *Don's Pearl*. From his earliest days as a saloonkeeper, every customer knew he placed a real pearl into every fifth *Don's Pearl*, and there was genuine excitement whenever a pearl was found. This new concept had the pearl inside an oyster inside an unopened tin can. He also supplied the can opener, and once the customer purchased the canned oyster, he or she could open it, dig into the oyster and remove the pearl.

Pearl cart outside Colonel's Plantation Beefsteak and Coffee House—International Market Place

Don the Beachcomber successfully operated the original pearl carts, called *Deep Sea Treasures*, at great profit for several years before he sold the operation to an independent investor at additional profit. Late in life Don said, *After all these years, this, what was to me a most ingenious idea, is still highly successful at the International Market Place, the Royal Hawaiian Shopping Center, Sea Life Park and shops throughout the islands.*

Honolulu City Hall was always Don the Beachcomber's number one nemesis, and he never seemed to escape the clutches of government. With his *Deep Sea Treasures* working so well, he took over two years to perfect a pineapple-juicing machine, and finding another machine that would cut away the hulls for sale to farmers as pig feed. This happened at a time when there was no such thing as fresh pineapple juice available in the islands. Even the pineapple juice sold by Dole was of the canned variety.

Pineapple cart outside Hyatt Hotel in Waikiki

The original plan was for a permanent open-air stand at the International Market Place that would dispense pineapple juice, sugar cane juice, macadamia nuts and fresh Kona coffee. Don drew up plans and made several fresh pineapple juice stands. These round structures were called *The Pineapple Tree*. Being portable, the kiosks could be placed anywhere along the sidewalk by franchised venders and easily rolled away at night. The first *Pineapple Tree* cart sat just outside the lobby entrance of the Hyatt Hotel along Kalakaua Avenue. Business was brisk, but it wasn't but a matter of days before the Board of Health swooped in and closed the operation down before it really got started. At the time city ordinances did not allow anyone to put a knife to any food sold outdoors in Honolulu.

# The State of Hawai`i

On April 25, 1957, The House of Representatives of the Territory of Hawai`i bestowed a very special honor upon Donn Beach a.k.a. Don the Beachcomber. House members adopted House Resolution No. 106 *Praising and Commending Don the Beachcomber for imagination, foresight and contribution to the development of tourism and urging him to continue romanticism, realism, color and charm in Hawai`i's tourist facilities*

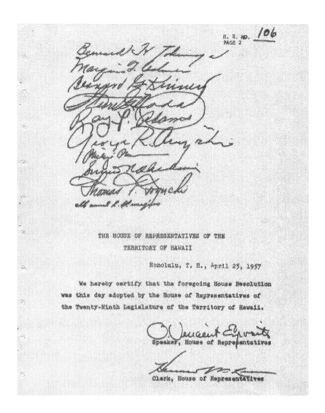

THE HOUSE OF REPRESENTATIVES OF THE
TERRITORY OF HAWAII

Honolulu, T. H., April 25, 1957

We hereby certify that the foregoing House Resolution
was this day adopted by the House of Representatives of
the Twenty-Ninth Legislature of the Territory of Hawaii.

Speaker, House of Representatives

Clerk, House of Representatives

Donn Beach's deep concern for the preservation of the Hawaiian culture, and restoration of the monarchy, led him to side with those who wanted self-rule. In 1959 with the outcome a seventeen to one majority in favor of statehood for Hawai`i, Donn Beach was one of the few to recognize the advantages a Limited Monarchy would bring. He could easily visualize the uncontrollable growth in population that statehood would bring, accompanied by undesirable outside influences. He felt it was necessary to retain the flavor of Hawai`i and the Polynesian ambiance so prevalent throughout the islands. In his opinion, it was of prime importance to a then budding tourist economy.

Once Hawai`i became the fiftieth state, he set his sights to make Waikiki a separate city in order to provide the optimum solution for the area. He lobbied the state legislature, and had legislation introduced to provide self-government for Waikiki.

*I sincerely felt the advantages would be better planning and zoning, which could be tailored to fit the specific needs of Waikiki. A faster and more reasonable response to the needs of the community was another benefit, along with the fact that a community with a governmental agency would be more effective when dealing with the State Legislature. This way, Waikiki could work in a more official manner to attract new business, and it would also have the ability to tax and keep the revenue in Waikiki where I felt it would do the most good. But the problem was, even by the time of statehood I realized, just as today, few really appreciated or understood Waikiki. While wanting growth in the tourist industry, I understood the beauty and fragility of Waikiki while appreciating its true possibilities for growth. The origin for my idea came because there was a need for controlled growth with total monitoring to maintain longevity in Waikiki's appeal to the rest of the world. Along with many others, I did not want Waikiki developed into a Miami style tourist Mecca, thus losing its Polynesian flavor and charm. However, this is exactly what has happened, and I am very disappointed with those who allowed the development. I have often said that, 'Hawai`i has been sold, but never really merchandised. We have the golden duck here, but we are squeezing the poor devil until there is almost nothing left.'*

Donn Beach's concern for the preservation of Hawai`i was expressed in many areas, and he constantly looked for ways to improve the ambiance of several unsightly sore spots around the island. He called Nimitz Highway between the Airport and Waikiki *"a mishmash of cars, chain-link fences, junk and additional eyesores."* With this area of town being the first visual impression for many visitors to Hawai`i, he led the fight for its cleanup. Donn even went out of his way to procure a lovely plant called Veronia elliptica, which grows like wildfire and looks like a cascade of jade, from Singapore and presented it to Paul Weissich of the Honolulu Botanic Gardens in order to see how it would grow in Hawai`i. With the assistance of Cliff Arquette of the Mayor's office, and the personal endorsement of Mayor Frank Fasi, a pilot program was approved. It then became a matter of getting approval from the state government to proceed.

In the end, Veronia elliptica was used only by Don the Beachcomber at the International Market Place. Eventually the Honolulu city government and some businesses along Nimitz Highway saw the light, and the appearance of this area improved to some degree.

# *Aku Aku*

Late in the same year, some old friends from Chicago called and invited Don the Beachcomber to Las Vegas. He was about to become involved in an exciting episode at the glamorous Stardust Hotel and Casino. At the first meeting with his old friends, he agreed to the position of advisor and consultant in the construction, decoration and operation of a Polynesian style restaurant to be called Aku Aku.

In this capacity, Don took with him as manager, his right-hand man in Waikiki, Benny Supnet. The Aku Aku turned out to be a beautiful Polynesian style restaurant, with a seating capacity of seven hundred, six Captains, twelve cooks, twenty-four waiters plus various other employees.

Just days after completion and the Grand Opening, a fire broke out in the employee kitchen in the middle of the dinner rush. The Aku Aku, filled almost to capacity with over six hundred dinner guests, was soon inundated with smoke.

When they evacuated the building, the employees were told to … *not worry about any money in the cash drawer, or any of the money they had collected during the evening and still held in their pockets."* The owners said, *"Just grab the dinner checks. Insurance covers everything.*

The restaurant was completely burned out and Donn was flown in from Honolulu once again for a high-level meeting with Al Benedict, John Dew and nine more hotel representatives. Discussions centered on one question. Why did Donn need to hire out-of-towners instead of locals, and what were their qualifications? He quickly explained about the current employee's knowledge of the type of food being served, and the service requirements, which would be next to impossible to teach novices in such a short time.

*I suggested to the hotel management that locals be slowly hired over a period of time, taught and worked into the natural employee turnover. In this manner they would learn from a very knowledgeable service staff that Benny Supnet and I had hand-picked especially for the Aku Aku and its unique and worldly clientele.*

The group fully understood and agreed with Donn's rationale. He was able to retain all of the employees who had started with the opening of the original Aku Aku, and kept on full salary ever since the fire.

While most of these employees made good money, their tips ranged from three hundred to four hundred dollars a night, some of them found it hard to save any money in Las Vegas. Eventually most of them returned to their homes in Los Angeles or Honolulu.

*What was my compensation, beside all expenses for two trips from Honolulu to Las Vegas and back? I departed Las Vegas at the end of each trip carrying a brown paper bag filled with fifty thousand dollars in cash.*

# Devil at Four o'clock

As time went by, Donn Beach's interests took him to other areas of the Pacific Rim on a regular basis. In April 1961 he sold the Don the Beachcomber Restaurant in the International Market Place to a hui headed up by Bob Hoffman, Kimo McVay, Sterling Mossman and his long-time friend, Duke Kahanamoku. The place was renamed Duke Kahanamoku's. But he continued to operate the Colonel's Plantation Beefsteak and Coffee House and Mandalay Room for a short time thereafter before he leased these food and drink operations to Christopher Hemmeter, then president of Associated Innkeepers, Inc.

*My favorite place, the 'Treehouse,' was retained as an office and private dinning room where I continued to entertain various guests and business associates while directing my operations. Eventually I sold the Hawai`i rights to the internationally known name—Don the Beachcomber—to a California business man who, in association with me, planned to opened Don the Beachcomber restaurants throughout the Hawaiian islands and the South Pacific.*

In the midst of all this change, Donn moved to Lahaina, Maui. One afternoon he received a call from a Hollywood producer friend inquiring about a location that would be a stand-in for Papeete for an up-coming television series based on the stories written by Jack London. There also had to be a hotel close by. *Well, I knew the exact location. Lahaina, Maui. Taking leave of Honolulu, I secured a fifty-year lease on the old Pioneer Inn.*

The sixteen-room Pioneer Inn, which had been built on the island of Lanai, had been cut in half and floated to Maui. This was where

Don the Beachcomber welcomed James Michener, who enjoyed a wonderful stay in room six, Queen Liliuokalani's haunt. While he lived here, Michener received unexpected inspiration in for his novel, *Hawai`i*.

On a cold, wind-chilled day in mid January, Donn's movie producer friend arrived with a full crew aboard a brigantine and tied up in front of the old hotel. With the Pioneer Inn as their base in Lahaina, three films were eventually made.

This cast and crew of the movie, *Devil at Four o'clock*, were constantly nourished with food and some of Don the Beachcomber's rhum concoctions at the new restaurant and bar in the hotel. As technical advisor on this movie, Donn had the opportunity to renew a relationship with an old acquaintance who he first met in Italy during World War II, Frank Sinatra.

The efforts of Donn Beach in Lahaina cannot be minimized. Here he was instrumental in getting the county of Maui to provide the proper safeguards for the restoration and retention of the flavor and old architecture of the town of Lahaina. He enlisted the assistance of Pete Wimberly, and obtained the necessary funds for plans for the historical restoration of this famous whaler's town through continuous lobbying efforts of the Legislature. In 1962, the county of Maui enacted ordinance number 321 which provided for the establishment of the Lahaina historical district.

# The Hong Kong Lady

*Standing on the forward upper deck overlooking the nighttime skyline of Singapore Harbor, a light easterly breeze whisked away the faint puffs of smoke from one my favorite Havana's, while my mind raced back over a lifetime of adventures, triumphs and disappointments. It was one of those rare moments of somber reflection I allowed myself when things went wrong. Flashes of the former Hong Kong Lady entered my head. These were memories of events not so long past when she had almost been torn apart shortly after her completion.*

In 1962, the *Hong Kong Lady*, a dream of Don the Beachcomber's for many years, began to take shape. At a cost of more than four million Hong Kong dollars, it would be a one hundred-fifty foot long Maharajah's version of a Mississippi riverboat, and it looked for all intents and purposes like success about to be launched. A deal, sealed only by a handshake with the governor of Hong Kong, Sir Robert Brown Black, had delivered the location for its berth near the British Yacht Club. Lease payment was to be ninety cents a month in perpetuity for a sight of four and one half acres. Also included in the deal was a hundred-fifty foot turn around area and a gaming concession, which was unusual because there was no gambling in Hong Kong. Governor Black enthusiastically agreed that the Hong Kong Lady, once in service as a unique and luxurious triple-deck floating restaurant and casino, would add great flavor to an already busy Hong Kong Harbor. The riverboat featured both public and private dinning rooms, bars and lounges and a coffee house. There was a formal dining room on the top deck and dance floor with a retractable roof. Guests could cruise the harbor at night and dance beneath the stars.

More than two hundred-fifty guests could be accommodated onboard the Lady. Menus embraced foods from many lands. From the Chinese broiler came Chinese pheasants. There were choice steaks from Omaha, baked potatoes from Idaho, salad greens from Hawai`i, fresh caught Hong Kong fish, lobster and prawns, and curries from India and Burma. Each day businessmen and visitors in the port could enjoy Don the Beachcomber's *Feast of the Islands* luncheon.

Hong Kong Lady depicted on fan in Hong Kong Harbor

To add to the attraction of the *Lady*, there would be daily fashion shows of fabrics and designs from Japan, China, India and other Far East countries.

Reminiscent of the old Mississippi River steamers in their glory days, the Hong Kong Lady would out do in plush elegance even the greatest of the American riverboats. She would ply the waters of Hong Kong harbor on a daily basis through a scene of hundreds of ferry boats, wallah wallahs, yachts, ocean liners from every port in the world, and warships of many nations, all in the harbor filled with excitement, the most colorful scene in the world.

The Beachcomber's Club, an exclusive private club, occupied half of the first deck. Here Don the Beachcomber would cater to the whims of international members and specialize in exotic and unusual food and drink creations.

Founder members of The Beachcomber's Club were issued a Beachcomber's Club Passport, not unlike a regular passport, with the Founder Member's photograph inside. The document detailed the member's rights and privileges, and included Donn's personalized red Chinese chop and his signature as Managing Director. On the last page there was the customary rendering of Don the Beach-comber in his Tahitian lauhala hat and an open khaki shirt.

Hong Kong Lady

A multilingual staff was hired to cater to each member's desires, and to assist members with personal shopping, sightseeing, local travel, and social and business arrangements.

Every detail of the Hong Kong Lady was designed for escapism, which Don the Beachcomber always believed everyone was looking for.

On Friday, May 26, 1961, the Headlines read *Hongkong Lady Shaping Up As Floating Palace.*

*Shortly after the christening and launching of my prized riverboat everything came to a sudden halt. I received the urgent call from my building manager while I was in Singapore. He told me the riverboat* had been lost in a hundred-twenty knot gale. A large wave had taken it from the docks and deposited it at the end of the airport, half in and half out of the water.

In the Far East there is a fruit, an unusual fruit, which is enjoyed and regarded as a delicacy by a great populace.

While Donn lived in Hong Kong he made several business trips to Singapore for various reasons. This is where he first learned about Durian. On this particular trip, he decided to acquire one of these fabulous fruits to take with him back to Hong Kong. It would be for any of his discriminating clientele at the Beachcomber's Club on the Hong Kong Lady.

*Upon receiving the bad news, I completed my business in Singapore, made the short trip to a local market to purchase the durian before I flew off to Hong Kong. I had carefully placed this exotic fruit into a brown paper bag and, thinking no more about it, I quickly boarded the aircraft, found my seat and stuffed the paper bag underneath.*

*The plane was about to taxi out from the tarmac onto the runway when the Captain announced there was a slight problem, and we would be turning back for the terminal area. He told his passengers to stay in our seats while the ground crew took care of the dilemma. At this, I opened a book I had stashed away in my briefcase, and settled in for the duration. My thoughts were on the Hong Kong Lady, and I took absolutely no notice of the confined space or the heat and the humidity within the plane's cabin. As time went by, I did not notice the disgusted looks of some of the other passengers.*

*Two hours later we were about to taxi out for takeoff when the Captain came barging into the cabin with a disgusted look of his own.*

*While its flavor is quite unique and extremely pleasant, and the fruit very palatable, durian can develop an extremely strong and offensive odor of an old abandoned toilet. By the time the Captain reached my seat towards the rear of the plane, the odor reeking out of the brown paper bag under my seat had permeated the entire plane. As for myself, I was completely oblivious to everything as I was deeply enthralled with my novel.*

*Arriving at my seat, the Captain, a friend of mine whom I had known for some years, looked down. Knowing my travel habits, he simply said, "Okay, Donn. Where do you have it?"*

*Eventually, we arrived in Hong Kong, and flying over Kai Tak airport I could easily see my pride and joy, The Hong Kong Lady, sitting at the end of the runway. Unable to move it due to its weight, the crew could only wait for a heavy tide. A few days later it came. To everyone's surprise the riverboat moved itself off the runway and back onto the water while at the same time crushing several smaller yachts beneath it.*

The dream of many years seemed ended. After another year and a half of struggles in the courts with the contractor and the insurance company, the new governor of Hong Kong, Sir David Crosbie Trench, venomously refused to honor his predecessor's handshake agreement on the gambling concession. The vessel was no longer economically viable for operation in the Crown Colony.

But, not all was lost for the *Hong Kong Lady*.

# The Singapore Lady

On the lookout for new funds and a new port of call for the *Hong Kong Lady*, Donn Beach turned to his good friend and associate, Bob Allen, President of the Hawai`i Visitors Bureau in Honolulu. Discussions of the problem led to Mr. Allen's connections in the Philippines.

*Bob suggested the two of us journey to Manila to look into the possibilities of setting up operations in the Bay of Cavite.*

*The Philippines were in quite a state of flux at the time. Lawlessness was the order of the day verging on descriptions akin to the early days of Dodge City, and with everyone carrying guns there were shootings in restaurants and hotels. Negotiations were already underway with a couple of the more powerful syndicates when I started snooping around the streets of Manila. I could easily sense the possibilities of what could happen to my investment if I brought it to Manila, even if I remained to watch over her. One morning when a shooting occurred in the lobby of my hotel, the Intercontinental, my rapidly developing fears of gangster connections were reinforced. Negotiations were broken off before noon, and Bob and I returned to Hong Kong on the very next plane.*

*The next port of call was Singapore and Tan Sri Khoo Tec Puat, the chairman of a Malaysian banking group in Singapore. Khoo was powerful in the community, and he felt the riverboat could be viable in Singapore Harbor. Khoo was also a good friend of the Premiere of Singapore, Mr. Lee Kuan Yew, and he felt a gaming concession would not be difficult to obtain. As Chairman of the Board of the Goodwood-Park Hotel, Khoo purchased my riverboat outright on behalf of the Corporation.*

Donn's battered riverboat, under new ownership, was now on its way to become the *Singapore Lady*, and Donn signed on to operate it at ten percent of the gross from food and liquor receipts, and twenty-five percent of the gaming profits.

The Singapore Lady

Resurrected, refitted and re-commissioned as the *Singapore Lady*, the beautiful riverboat was finally able to ply her trade and wares in a fashion suitable for a Maharajah. Donn designed small, attractive launches to ferry passengers to and from the restaurant. These launches, a novelty, added to the glamour of the entire operation.

*With the gaming equipment ordered, Khoo and Singapore's Premiere, Lee Kuan Yew, got into an argument that almost developed into a full-blown fistfight. In the end, the Premiere refused to issue the private gaming license. The Singapore Lady operated successfully as a showtime restaurant out of Clifford Pier for several years thereafter.*

*When I stepped off the deck of my creation for the final time, I was satisfied my dream had come to a successful conclusion. Now I was on my way to the next appointment. The Sultan of Brunei awaited my consultation.*

# A Zillion Dollar Idea

Late in 1964 when he returned to Saigon on his way from Brunei to Honolulu, Donn stopped in Singapore at one of his favorite hotels, the old Raffles. When he dropped by the newsstand kiosk for a supply of paperbacks for his return flight, he noticed one published in Australia. It was a book had written by two Australian Army Captains after their escape in 1942 from the infamous Changi Prison on the outskirts of Singapore.

The story described their escape from Changi during an electrical thunderstorm. It seems they were near a rear gate when a heavy rained caused a temporary blackout, and made it possible for them to crawl under a fence where the rain had washed a trench sufficient for their size.

The Captains had not planned for such an opportunity, and had not prepared any food or other essentials necessary for an escape. However, they did have a small compass, and they headed in the general direction of Sumatra. They had learned while in prison that there was an Australian naval unit somewhere in the Torres Straits.

For four days, they tramped through the jungles and stopped at several villages to try to obtain food and directions. On the fifth day, they approached yet another village, but the headman quickly ran out to wave them away. He said a Japanese unit was nearby in search of escaped prisoners, and if any were found in the village, the people of the village would be shot.

The two men had managed to find some fruit, roots and nuts along the way, but they were weak, and quite starved. Eventually they became dizzy, and decided to stop by a stream to rest and quench their thirst. Of course, they fell asleep and later awaken somewhat startled by fruit that dropped on their faces. Large birds fed above them.

The army Captains tasted the fallen fruit, reasoned that if it was safe enough for the birds to eat, then they would be in no danger. Therefore, they proceeded to stuff their bellies with the purple, plum-like fruit, and drank from the nearby stream.

Again, they slept, only to be awakened about midnight with a start to discover they both had a throbbing erection. They started to laugh at the ridiculousness of their situation, and in an attempt to alleviate their condition they stripped off their old khaki shorts and plunged into the stream. The bizarre condition subsided.

*At this point in their story, I got what I believed to be a 'Zillion Dollar Idea.' What was in the purple fruit they had eaten? I had to investigate.*

During their journey through the jungle, the two men had discovered, after many enquiries that the name of the fruit was *Gandarookem*. The villagers explained that the fruit was to be found in Sumatra, Java and Bali. This was all the information Donn Beach needed.

With Bali on his way to Honolulu, Donn stopped over and visited with a delightful couple who owned a charming thatched bungalow on Sanur Beach. Over dinner on the first night, he queried them about the *Magic Fruit*. Rumors circulated that President Sukarno had the trees in his garden so he could enjoyed the fruit, and often gave it to friends. His reputation as a lady's man seemed to bear out the efficacy of *Gandarookem*.

*The next morning my host drove me up in the hills back of Sanur where we located some of these special trees. We took about a quart of the half ripened fruit.*

*I departed for Honolulu with my treasure safely packed in plastic bags for easy smuggling in my pockets through Honolulu customs. Having reached home, and with my treasures safely tucked away in my refrigerator, I knew I must find out if the fruit would be absolutely safe to package and to sell to the waiting world. I called the manager of a well-known testing laboratory in Los Angeles and asked him to analyze a quantity that I was mailing to him. I wanted him to look for any harmful or dangerous properties the fruit might have. He called me a couple of weeks later and stated that he needed more samples as most of the sample had rotted in transit. This was a blow, so I decided to test the balance in my refrigerator on myself.*

*One evening after two martinis to give me courage, I sat down and ate the whole lot. This constituted of about a pint, the last of the Gandarookem.*

*I waited for about three hours, hoping the Aussie Captains' effect would become apparent. It might have been wishful thinking on my part, or auto-suggestion, but I did experience a feeling of euphoria, and a half an erection did appear. The next morning no side effects were obvious. I was convinced I had a Winnah.*

*I had planned to return to Singapore to do some consulting for the Tourist Department of the Government of Singapore, and I stopped in Sumatra to take up the trail of Gandarookem supplies. I located my nephew near Medang, and we took off for the jungles. We found a great number of trees loaded down with the fruit. I arranged for my nephew to pack and ship about five pounds to me when I returned to Honolulu. My nephew would now act as my agent in Sumatra, Java and Bali, supplying my requirements.*

*Some days after my return to Honolulu I received a telephone call from the agent in charge of the Hawai`i Agriculture Department requesting that I come down and talk with him about a shipment of fruit that had arrived that day. In his office, he asked me to identify the fruit. I could only tell him a friend had sent me a gift, whereupon the agent explained he would have to destroy the entire shipment. After much argument, I asked him if I could put the contents of the shipment* *through a blender and take it home with me. He agreed to this, so I hurriedly returned home to collect my high-speed blender and some jars and returned to the agent's office. I went home pleased with myself and put the jars filled with puree into my refrigerator.*

*To prepare the fruit for use, my idea was to boil the puree to a pulp and make a liqueur. This I did. The result was two quarts of delicious tasting, syrupy liquid.*

*My next idea was to use the magic syrup as the filling for a chocolate candy. I had enjoyed similar confections filled with Benedictine, so to me this seemed the perfect way to dispense and market my potent elixir.*

*After several experiments, and finding the candy that suited the product, the problem was where, and to whom to market it. I decided to make up some samples and take them to owners of boutiques. At this point I could not prove or disprove that the chocolates contained a sufficient quantity of the supposed aphrodisiac, nor could I determine the required number of chocolates to be consumed to provide the hoped for effects.*

*Bag in hand, I approached another friend who owned and operated a very exclusive boutique in Beverly Hills. I explained my mission and showed her the beautiful box of my special chocolates where upon she shouted, "Eureka! You have found the fountain of youth!" She immediately wanted to place a large order for her wealthy clientele, and other possible outlets she had in mind as well.*

*I gave this enthusiastic and potential customer a box of samples. I also gave samples to two other purveyors and requested they take them home to experiment with their husbands or lovers. They agreed to do so, and to describe the results a few days later.*

*My hopes became somewhat dashed on hearing the testimonials I had so eagerly awaited. I had asked the boutique owner not inform her husband of the contents of the candy. She said they ate several pieces of the delicious confection, and apart from feeling warm and flushed and a lit-*

*tle nauseated, nothing else was apparent. Our tests had not been encouraging.*

*A few weeks later, I received a call from an oriental gentleman who explained that he was the major importer and exporter of exotic herbs, and he wanted to acquire the exclusive distribution in the Far East. The sum he suggested for this was staggering, "But," he added. "We must provide proof that the mysterious fruit worked.*

*At this point, we had exhausted my little supply of Gandarookem with zero success, so I re-read the Aussie Captains' book to see if I had missed something. The answer came to me in a flash of common sense.*

*An excessive intake of water in a weakened condition, for a man, could only result in the natural, but sometimes-alarming situation such as the Captains had found themselves.*

*Now I felt much better. I hadn't lost a Zillion dollars.*

# The Pacific Rim

Always aware of the environment and ambiance of the tourist destination, Hawai`i, and the invasion of greed he saw in the islands, Donn Beach once wrote: *It is sad but true that a great many of the present day visitors to Hawai`i, especially Waikiki, depart our shores with a feeling of being cheated and disillusioned. One of the reasons is that there is entirely too much emphasis on mediocrity. It would appear very little thought or consideration is given to the fact that the average visitor is seeking and expecting a fulfillment of his or her South Sea island dream—not sleek modernity no matter how elegant and symbolic. The visitor also wants comfort along with adventure. This can be given in a colorful and exciting Polynesian wrap, and a happy visitor, thoroughly enjoying their stay, who gets what they came for will go home an enthusiastic booster of Hawai`i, which is or should be the goal of all in the field of tourism in Hawai`i.*

Convinced of the tremendous area of opportunity for the development of tourism throughout the *Pacific Rim*, Donn Beach expanded his *Blue Lagoon Development Company* from an import/export business. Now he began to devote most of his time, energy and expertise to the development of new, exciting and unusual tourist attractions, not only in Hawai`i, but in the Pacific-Asian area as well. All of the projects he worked on would contribute to the overall development of romanticism, realism, color, flavor, charm, showmanship and authenticity of the area's culture, and give any vacation destination a certain magical charm offered nowhere else. With the advent of faster air travel throughout the world, tourism started to become a major business in any country able to offer attractive vacations to visitors. Donn Beach believed it to be of ever-increasing importance to provide certain expected attractions in order to meet the expectations of a more discerning traveler. Further, he felt Pacific-Asian countries desirous of being able to attract overseas visitors should make concessions to operators highly experienced in the development of tourism, and to be able to make first-class, colorful presentations to those travelers.

*In other words, to clean up their acts.*

Donn Beach at Waiakea Resort—Hilo, Hawai`i—Big Island

Hired by C. Brewer as a Consultant, Donn orchestrated various elements, including the colorful Market Place in their twelve million dollar Waiakea Village Resort in Hilo on the island of Hawai`i. Donn found new ways to turn adventure and romance into dollars and cents, on behalf of C. Brewer. He was sent across the South

Pacific, to the Far East and India to purchase, import and set-up a constant supply of attractive items and trade goods for the shops in the Waiakea Village Market Place. Such unusual items included grains of rice incased in glass with the Lord's Prayer or words of Mao Tes-Tung inscribed on them. There were fine silks from Thailand, sugar-crushing machines from Singapore for fresh sugar juice.

As a result of his trip to Manila in search of a new home for his Hong Kong Lady, Donn and Bob Allen were welcomed with open arms by Delfin Montano, Provincial Governor of the City of Cavite. Here he was appointed as Tourist Consultant to the Province of Cavite. The history of Cavite goes back to the days when Spain ruled over the Philippines where the Spanish built several beautiful churches and gave the town its own unique ambience.

In the capacity of Tourist Consultant, Donn Beach worked on many projects, the principle one being the restoration of the old Spanish walled fort which had been bombed out of existence on December 10, 1941, and the establishment of museum sites to recreate the City of Cavite as the *Home of the Galleons*. The goal of this project was to make Cavite Province a prime tourist destination. Cavite was the birthplace of the gold and silver fleets bound for Spain, and in development of this tourist attraction, three of the sunken Spanish Galleons were discovered.

Over the years, Bob Allen, Pete Wimberly and Donn Beach combined their talents to bring about a number of successful enterprises in such places as Kuala Terengganu, Kota Kinabalu in Borneo, and Brunei.

*One of these was called Malaysia in Miniature. The project was about twenty miles from the capitol of Malaysia, Kuala Lumpua. The developer, Dato Teh Hong Piow, a local banker, with influence from Pete Wimberly and myself, designed an amusement park in three hundred acres of semi-jungle. The original concept called for a Malay village where natives would live and perform during the daytime. There were daily exhibits of local arts and craft, native foods, spears and war clubs as well as live demonstrations of their ever-dangerous blowgun.*

# The Marama

The name *Marama*, which means *The Far Seeing*, and was bestowed upon Don the Beachcomber earlier in his life by an old Tahitian woman. The inspiration behind all of his ideas sprang from decades of observant travel in the globe's most exotic locales. It all started when he first visited the pristine shores of Tahiti in 1929 where he fell in love with the Pacific Islands.

Almost fifty years later, the *Marama*, a daydream inspired on a visit to another of his favorite places, Aitutaki in the Cook Islands, a place he called, *The last bit of paradise on earth*, would come true. While he relaxed offshore in a small single outrigger canoe, Donn was struck by the obvious, ... *that a palm-lined white sand beach beneath towering green mountains is best appreciated from a perspective of one hundred yards offshore in the cool mosquito-free lagoon breezes.*

The Marama in a tropical lagoon in Tahiti

Conventional hotels or resort construction would mar the primeval beauty of such a landscape. But Donn felt a floating Polynesian style hotel room could preserve the unspoiled view while it contained every amenity for the vacationer. When he returned to Honolulu, he sat down with his good friend, Herb Kane. With rhum punches close at hand, and Herb, President of the Polynesian Voyaging Society drawing sketches, Don the Beachcomber described his dream.

The genesis of the *Marama* was the Blue Lagoon Fa're, a Tahitian thatched hut (fa're) mounted on twin canoe hulls to resemble an ancient Polynesian double canoe. Complete with a self-contained fresh water system and an ecologically pure sanitation system, flotillas of these fa'res would be built and anchored in the tropical lagoons of Bora Bora and Moorea, the Sea of Cortez, the Caribbean and in other pleasant and placid blue lagoons just made for escape. They would be designed to be exclusive for a romantic twosome, yet twenty friends could be easily entertained on the ample deck and the roomy Tahitian salon.

With a weight in excess of ten tons and a length of forty-three foot, the first fa're was exceptionally stable. Deck space was over eight hundred square feet. Taking seven months to build, Donn decorated the interior with materials gathered from the Pacific Islands and Asia. The Fa're was luxuriously appointed with mahogany and teakwood, capiz shell walls, sea shell lighting, panels of bamboo with a woven pandanus ceiling. The kitchen and bar were fully equipped as were the bedroom, bath and shower. An independent electrical power system was also built in. The glass topped table inside the Tahitian salon was used for dining, or as a place to set a refreshing rhum drink. The same glass top also afforded a view into the depths below to watch the activities of exotic multi-colored fish and other marine creatures. Powerful floodlights illuminated the waters to view at night, and should a lobster or an especially succulent fish come into view, the tabletop lifted off so that one could attempt to spear or net at will.

To compliment the fa're, Don the Beachcomber planned shore facilities with restaurants and shops. For those who would rather stay on board, pareu-clad lovelies paddled alongside each morning to vend fresh fish, fruits and flowers. The fa're also came with a small outrigger canoe for transportation to shore.

*My original creation was docked at Keehi Lagoon where friends and business associates visited and enjoyed afternoon and evening rhum punches like my original 'Marama Rhum Punch.' My attempted to install this revolutionary idea in Honolulu proved more than frustrating to say the least. Plans for several fa'res along the Waikiki shoreline as rental units for the more adventurous visitor to the islands was set adrift once again by city hall.*

Donn sat the *Marama* onboard the deck of the Matson Steamship Mariposa and took his much admired and prized possession to Tahiti where it was docked at a jetty along side the bungalows of the Beachcomber Hotel in Papeete. When new management took over the hotel, he moved the *Marama* across the channel to the blue lagoon of Moorea. Insurance coverage proved difficult to obtain, as the French insurance companies could not determine if the *Marama* was a house or a boat. There was no such thing as a houseboat in Tahiti. Without insurance, the concept became infeasible, but Don the Beachcomber enjoyed his life of a beachcomber on board the *Marama* for several years until the dream ended when a series of three violent hurricanes hit in rapid succession with no time for repairs. In the end, the third hurricane was too much for the *Marama* to handle.

# Singapore

From his early days of travel on the Asian continent, Singapore had always left Don the Beachcomber with a feeling that he had been in an old dilapidated, decayed, smelly village. Arrival into Singapore through an airport littered with trash and garbage was bad enough, but to have this atmosphere continue throughout the country was a situation impossible to tolerate. He recognized Singapore's potential, made shrewd observations and compared Singapore to such places as Hong Kong, Japan. Then, he outlined a draft to Dr. Goh Keng Swee, Minister for Finance of Singapore, and provided assistance for improvements that could lead to an enjoyable experience for future visitors.

*I profiled various areas where enhancements to the city could be made, such as, the airport and shopping areas. Refuse and garbage was a prime candidate for improvement. In many areas, visitors were exposed to rotting garbage and stench from refuse in water drains. I encouraged strict government enforcement of sanitary laws. The shops on many of the main and busy streets such as Orchard Road were in dilapidated condition. Walls were moldy and very unsightly, and I suggested cash prizes be awarded to business establishments that created the most attractive shops. Other prizes were to be awarded for the best-kept gardens, the best-looking homes, etc. Anyone looking around Singapore today will notice these suggestions were not taken with a grain of salt as Singapore is one of the cleanest countries in the world. When I suggested that pastel colors be used, and Singapore should be developed as a showcase of experiences most pleasing to the eye, the Minister took notice. I knew overseas visitors would expect to see lush tropical plantings and gardens so I suggested hotel owners and developers provide the money to plant mature Queen Palms, Travelers Palms and other exotic flowering trees on their properties. I also suggested to Mr. Tan Sri Khoo that the drive of the Malaysia Hotel be lined with twenty Queen Palms in a stately line from the entrance of the property thus providing a grand vehicular entrance.*

Over time, Donn made many suggestions to the Singapore government, most of which they followed through on. His suggestions covered the gammut. Included were ideas for the various small islands like Sentosa, and finally the waterfront. Here a floating restaurant, *The Singapore Lady*, became a beautiful and colorful attraction for local residents and visitors to the small industrious nation.

*Years later, when I arrived at the Changi International Airport in Singapore I was thrilled to see the enhancements to the stark grey concrete walls. Not only were they accented with brilliant green ferns throughout, but the soft sounds of cool waterfalls blanketed the senses with a feeling of calmness and delight. A community of airport workers had achieved a sense of pride, and the overall visual effects were not unappreciated. Driving into the city along the boulevard, I could see the manicured medium strip lined with colorful and beautifully trimmed Shower trees. The arriving visitor felt more than welcomed, and the overall effect created expectations of things to come.*

# Don the Beachcomber's Fertile Mind

There were numerous projects which Don the Beachcomber became involved in over the years. Projects like the *Beachcomber Cabaret-Restaurant Under the Sea* to be built a short distance off the shoreline of Rockefeller properties on the island of Hawai`i. Another project to be called the *Beachcomber's Village* on the island of Lanai would offer one hundred native style bungalows constructed of native materials such as ohia timber, lauhala matted walls, thatched roofs, with another one hundred for use as rental units. Included would be restaurants, shops, a night club, luau grounds, a drugstore and other amenities to meet all of the resident and visitor needs. He developed these ideas before the filming of the movie, Hawai`i, realizing that upon the movie's release, thousands of additional visitors would be attracted to the islands. The new visitors to Hawai`i would look for an image not offered in Waikiki, with its noise, modern shops, crowded narrow beaches, traffic congestion and concrete towers. The *Beachcombers Village on Pineapple Island* was designed to reflect the essence, charm and flavor of old Hawai`i as dramatized in James Michener's epic.

Don the Beachcomber on the beach

As every good entrepreneur knows, not all ideas come to pass. Although many of his new and radical ideas never reached maturity, Don the Beachcomber's mind never relaxed.

As an example, there was the railway system for Kaanapali on the island Maui, and the motorized San Francisco style cable cars for all islands.

In New Zealand, he proposed utilization of indigenous culture for hotel decoration and entertainment at a time when there was no such thing. At the same time, his proposal for private gaming clubs in Auckland created a great deal of interest.

*Feeling the country was ripe, ready and willing for expansion of its tourist industry, I proposed, designed and promoted a thirty-million-dollar resort for the Bay of Islands.*

Two other resorts were proposed and designed, one at Matauri Bay and another at Takou Bay with an enlarged airport in Kerikeri. The thought of attracting a broader range of international visitors to the *Land of the Long White Cloud*, and in particular to the North Island, encountered such stiff resistance that Donn Beach just plain gave up on any idea of expansion of tourism development in New Zealand. It was beyond his imagination why the people of any country who starved for a new, strong source of revenue would deliberately turn their backs on such a valuable resource.

While living in the Cook Islands in the 1970's, Donn came upon something very unexpected while visiting the motu of Mauke and the motu of Mitiaro.

Among the banana orchards this unexpected discovery grew wild and was a problem weed to the Cook Islanders who whacked away at the bushy pest with machetes. To Donn, the *maile* vines were immediately recognizable as a godsend for the Hawaiian floral industry.

*Originating this new industry became an education in itself for all concerned. First of all the I found myself devoting much of my time and energy working with the women of the Cook Islands in order to instruct them in the art of making maile leis. First, there was the gathering of the maile (maire in the Cook Islands) from deep within the makatea (an up-lifted coral reef) amid shrubs, sharp rock and coral. Next, there was the business end of the new enterprise. Things such as deadlines were foreign to these women. Then, there was quality control and consistency in the product being produced. To finish off their education, packing and ship-ping details were taught along with a valuable education in intricacies of transportation from distributor to distributor. Financial reimbursement rounded out the list. Years later, thanks to the education I had provided my employees, these same women brought the maile operation to a stand-still with a work stoppage. This happened when the new operators who had taken over the business refused to pay these same women who so readily supplied them with their valuable commodity.*

*Although Cook Island maile has less fragrance when fresh, it is a much fuller plant than the variety grown in Hawai`i. Even today, maile grown in the Hawaiian Islands is difficult to access, and not enough of it can be picked to keep up with the demand.*

Because of Donn Beach's foresight, his efforts were not unre-warded. By the early 1980's over five hundred maile leis arrived at the Honolulu International Airport every week for sale to local flo-rists.

He crisscrossed the Pacific numerous times and developed the merchandising format and purchased items for the *Cultural Center and Market Place at Pacific Harbour* in Fiji. He acted as consultant to resort developers and created new and viable attractions at Raro-tonga in the Cook Islands, Tahiti, Samoa, Tonga and the Marshall Islands as well as Pago Pago, American Samoa and Vanuatu. For the Saltan of Brunei, he developed the concept and plans for a fifty pas-senger river craft for visitors to travel up-country to meet and view the unique hill tribes.

One of his last projects was the Aloha Skyway, a monorail system for the city of Honolulu to help relieve the congestion of crowded city streets.

# *Only One Don the Beachcomber*

In 1989 when Donn Beach, a.k.a. Don the Beachcomber, finally decided to scrounge beaches of other worlds, he left behind a legacy and a gift for anyone to use, a foundation for others to build upon. It was once said of Donn Beach, that ... *he has probably done more as a single person for tourism in Hawai`i and nations of the Pacific Rim than any other.*

Donn Beach—a.k.a. Don the Beachcomber

The numerous newspaper and magazine articles written in the local community in Hawai`i, and the newspaper and magazine articles written by the international press about Don the Beachcomber will attest to that.

Many businessmen and businesswomen in Hawai`i and throughout Polynesia and the Pacific Rim nations have prospered as a direct result of the ingenious foresight and innovative ideas brought forth by Don the Beachcomber. From even the earliest days of his illustrious career, copy cats took every opportunity to whisk away any original concept he had to offer, often times they claimed as their own. Nevertheless, even though Don the Beachcomber found it personally difficult to chase after these copy cats, for it just wasn't within him to take any form of retribution on anyone, these people unknowingly only helped to add to the luster, mystique and leadership of this colorful personality.

Someday someone will come along who has read about or heard about Don the Beachcomber, and they may even think this person was nothing more that a myth, as did syndicated columnist Jim Bishop. This individual may even attempt to re-invent the man and the myth who created so many original and successful concepts. These started with his grass shacks and Sunday evening luau in the heart of Waikiki and his Encino Plantation. However, they will never succeed. For you see, there will only be one Don the Beachcomber. He was just too much of a honest to goodness good human being for it to happen again.

From rhum punches on McCadden Street to bush beer and tropical nights on Aitutaki, to a floating fa're in the tropical lagoons of French Polynesia, adventure, romance, soft music and lovely maidens were always close by, with the Diplomats, Beachcombers, Princes and Pirates never far behind.

With the passing of Donn Beach, a.k.a. Don the Beachcomber, and others of the same generation, we now find an era of gentility has vanished from the face of the earth.

# From the files of Donn Beach—Author Unknown

### Don the Beachcomber

Affable host, nervous gait, independent and charming rake.
Preoccupied, truantly shy, rhum drinks he'll glorify.
Up and down a jumping Jack, a half smiling demoniac.
Tuberoses, an odorous lei, round his neck will proudly sway.
A lofty brow, a pointed ear, a globe trotting Mutineer.
Restless soul, much ado, scent of copra his taboo.
Libations of golden rhum, secret passion a native drum.
His carnal joy a bloody light, red against the inky night.
Confoundedly ever polite, intelligentsia, his delight.
Polite chatter to one and all, sensitive and whimsical.
Cryptic eyes too alert, for idle ladies that love to flirt.
Melancholia colorful mood, lover of dank solitude.
His only torch a tropic isle, me thinks,
A silhouette in bowels of night,
Don The Beachcomber the satellite.
Ah, shrewd wastrel of business first, thy soul will ever be accursed.
The mystic longing in thy breast, will never give thee any rest.
A tropic sun will keep thee always on the run.
A blue lagoon, a tortured drum, to those eternally wilt thou
succumb.

Thy ruby blood in limpid vein, will long again for blitzkrieg rain.

Off you go, another shore. Peace for thee, ah, nevermore.

Intangible and wishful male, thus you stand with randed veil.

Of willing brain thy soul has known a sea of pain.

Introvert of island fame, thy Hut will always win acclaim.

Succulent shrimp plus gourmet grub, will always fill your cozy club.

And rhum alone in gloried style, will always beckon and beguile.

So carry on, you'll do alright.

Thou enigmatic water sprite.

Sail off with copra to tropic joy, thou brown eyes, winsome, illusive boy.

And when you lounge 'neath drooping frond, dream of Hollywood, oh vagabond.

As in a mist behold the place, that gave your name it fetching grace.

Behold the din, the fleeing mortals, mad escapists, at your portals.

Then laugh at them, the gruesome crowd, laugh at them.

Yeah, long and hard, for there art thou in paradise.

Yes, Don the man I immortalize.

Don Desperado, by gad, by damn, who will always take it on the lam.

And may you thrive and purple grapes, thou silent, sinister, Jack-a-napes.

So ship-a-hoy, and fare-thee-well, from a nervy Demoiselle.

And that's the end of this verse,

of a drifter with a drifter's curse.

On June 7, 1989 when the essence that was Donn Beach, a.k.a. Don the Beachcomber left this earthly environment, he had outlived all other members of his immediately family other than his wife, Phoebe. But, those who mourned his passing were there. For you see, not only did The Beachcomber leave behind many of his thoughts, dreams, ideas and accomplishments for others to use and build on, he also left behind a living legacy of more than two thousand friends who came to the funeral services at the Punchbowl National Cemetery of the Pacific. These were some of the many who had worked with, had gained experience from, and had benefitted from his friendship, his guidance and his remarkable energy and ingenious foresight.

This demonstration of affection came from the heart of each individual, and there were many more around the world who could not attend, but who sent their condolences. This was to be their final tribute to a man who had meant so much to each of them.

## The End

978-0-595-47884-2
0-595-47884-0

www.ingramcontent.com/pod-product-compliance
Lightning Source LLC
Chambersburg PA
CBHW051243050326
40689CB00007B/1050